{ A FLAME FOR THE LORD }

The Life of Mother Kolumba Białecka

Foundress of the Congregation
of the Sisters of St. Dominic

BY SR. M. FELICITY WOLF, O.P.

Table of Contents

Introduction

The book you take into your hands is the very first English biography of a humble Polish woman whose vision, determination and exemplary love for Christ and his people, especially those in need, gave birth to the religious Congregation of the Sisters of Saint Dominic.

For those who still find interest in reading biographies of spiritual giants, declared or not yet declared by the Church as saints, the reading of this book should be a quite enlightening and inspiring experience. The author of this book presents the life of Mother Kolumba Białecka with great insight and due respect for the well-documented testimonies of people who knew this remarkable woman and felt compelled to share with others their personal observations of her life. This was a life profoundly immersed in, focused on and motivated by the reality of Christ's presence in the Sacrament of the Holy Eucharist. Mother Kolumba's extraordinary devotion to the Eucharistic Lord was the heartbeat and the driving force of her spirituality, which enabled her to see the depth of the spiritual and physical needs of her contemporaries and compelled her to respond to them with great vision, love, enthusiasm and perseverance. The founding of a religious congregation with its specific charism requires not only a clear vision of its place and role in the world and an outstanding ability to discern God's plan for it, but also heroic courage and reliance on his guidance and protection. Mother Kolumba found the source of all these in her profound devotion to Christ in the Holy Eucharist.

Today, in the early years of the twenty-first century, we find ourselves in critical and urgent need of deepening our appreciation for the greatest sacrament of the Church – the Holy Eucharist – and rekindling a faith-shaping devotion to it. I hope this book will help us to rediscover the immensity of Christ's love manifested in his Eucharistic presence, encourage us to intensify our personal relationship with Him, and prompt us to a more generous and loving response to the material and spiritual needs of others.

I recommend this book out of gratitude to its author and editor, and with the hope that it will find its way not only into the hands of those who responded to Christ's call to the consecrated life but also into the hands of all those who take seriously God's call to holiness and seek inspiration, guidance and encouragement for their spiritual endeavors, and remain determined to live and proclaim their Catholic faith effectively and joyfully in acts of genuine devotion and deeds of charity.

Mother M. Natalie Pekala, O.P.
Provincial Superior
Dominican Sisters, Immaculate Conception Province
November 2020

Prologue

Enter a darkened Catholic church, and you may see a solid red glow to the center or side. Stronger than any exit sign or security system, this eerie light should not alarm. It is a sanctuary lamp, whose constant burning reminds Catholics that Jesus Himself is present in the tabernacle, burning with love for us.

Some sanctuary lamps today are electric; others are fed by the measured burning of paraffin candles. But anyone who has seen a beeswax candle burn itself out before the Blessed Sacrament will notice a difference: a vibrant, leaping light. With wick untrimmed, the wax melts faster and faster, the flame jumps higher and higher, and it seems as though the candle cannot wait to exhaust itself completely.

Those who knew Kolumba Białecka compared her to such a lamp, burning with love for the Blessed Sacrament, unquenchable in her desire to exhaust herself for Christ. Like a sanctuary light, her very existence revolved around Jesus' Presence in the tabernacle. But, remarkably for a religious woman of her society, Mother Kolumba did not stay sequestered near the sanctuary. She poured herself into founding a contemplative-active group of sisters to bring the truth of Jesus Christ out of the church into homes and schools—and so to draw others back to Truth itself, Christ in the Eucharist.

Even though tuberculosis plagued Róża (Kolumba) Białecka[1] from when she was young, she did not use poor health as an excuse to conserve her strength and exert herself in careful, restricted measure. She deliberately gave everything to fulfilling God's will for her life. At age seventeen[2], she agreed to found the Sisters of St. Dominic in Poland because she understood this to be God's will; at age forty-one, she agreed to resume leadership of the Congregation for the same reason—although she knew it meant "sacrificing her health and life."[3] By age forty-eight, Mother Kolumba Białecka had completely expended herself to establish and consolidate this foundation of Dominican sisters. She used every last ounce of energy to prepare her sisters to preach the Truth of the Gospel by their lives. Consequently, much of her life story is told in the lessons she gave her sisters; but we cannot dismiss it as relevant only to them. All Christians are called to cultivate faith, zeal, love, self-sacrifice, pure intentions, and so much more, as Mother Kolumba did. As Cardinal Grocholewski, the Prefect of the Congregation for Catholic Education, exclaimed upon hearing of Mother's devotion to the Eucharist: "This! This is important today.

---

[1]Polish version of Rose, pronounced *Roojzha*. Kolumba was the name she received in the convent, see Ch. 2. A Polish surname often ends in "a" when belonging to a woman but changes to "i" for men; hence her father's surname was Białecki; Białecka is pronounced *Beah*-WETZ-*ka*.

[2]Although ages in Poland are considered increased at the turn of the year, they have been adjusted in this work to account for the American system of "turning older" on one's birthday—and Róża Białecka was born in August 1838. So, for example, she is considered in American terms to have been 11 years old in the spring of 1850, whereas Polish sources describe her as 12.

[3]Benwenuta Pasławska, O.P., *The Life of Reverend Mother Róża Kolumba Białecka*, Publishing House of the Discalced Carmelites, Kraków, 2007, Ch. XV. Hereafter cited as *Life*.

We must underscore this nowadays."[4] Mother Kolumba's fire for the Eucharist should ignite a spark in us all. Imitating her, we can find fuel in the Eucharist to exercise virtue in daily challenges.

Reader, beware: the testimony of saintly lives can often lead us to believe that we can't hold a candle to them. Next to the leaping lights, we appear as tiny tapers or begrudging, self-conserving paraffin candles. What talents do we have, and how could we possibly expend them with no thought for ourselves? But the challenge of Mother Kolumba's life is precisely this: she was not especially trained or well-equipped, super saintly or without spiritual struggles. Rather, God gave her the qualities, helps and, yes, even the challenges she needed to become holy. The one thing that may set Mother Kolumba Białecka apart from us are the choices she made to cooperate with God's grace and tenaciously, generously, daily, pursue His Plan. The truly challenging truth? Nothing keeps us from doing the same.

---

[4]Quoted by Mother Julia Bakalarz, O.P., in her address to the Sisters of St. Dominic, "Vocation to the Eucharistic Life of the Lord's Servant Mother Kolumba Białecka in Light of Holy Father John Paul II's Teaching of the Eucharist" delivered in symposium "…So That Christ Could Live within Me from Now On," Kraków, Feb. 11-12, 2005.

Chapter 1
FOUNDATIONAL INFLUENCES

Parents are often a significant, if hidden, ingredient in the makings of a saint, and Róża's parents deserve due recognition. Anna Ernestyna and Franciszek Białecki were Polish gentry who lived their faith and passed it on to their three daughters. When Róża was born in 1838, the middle of the surviving children, the Białeckis lived on Anna Ernestyna's estate in Galicia, now Ukrainian territory. At the time, the area belonged to the Austro-Hungarian empire. Three neighboring powers—Russia, Prussia and Austria—had completed their partitioning of Poland in 1795. Even though Poland had officially ceased to exist some forty years before Róża's birth, inhabitants of Galicia identified as Polish, and religious expressions often became political statements.

But the Białeckis taught Róża a faith that went deeper than politics. They participated in public events such as church fairs and parish missions, it is true, but they cultivated the faith in private ways as well. Their home chapel was frequented through devotional practices and house meetings. The Białeckis prayed the rosary regularly, and Róża's mother taught her how to talk to Christ at a young age. One

The Białecki manor, no longer standing, included a family chapel.

anecdote recalls Róża's fondness for the rosary: she would encourage her younger sister to say it with her, but Władzia preferred a much more rapid pace. So Róża suggested a compromise that would not interrupt the prayer. "When I speak too slowly, just touch me with your hand, Władzia," she said, "and when you speak too fast I will do it myself."[5]

Róża found great joy in prayer, understanding it to be a conversation with God that was not limited to specific times but could change its form throughout the day.[6] By eight years old, she already enjoyed being alone with Christ, and could talk with Him without end. Róża's love of prayer would stand her in good stead through the ups and downs of her life.

Some years before Róża's life began, the Jesuit order had been expulsed from Russia and the Białeckis had welcomed these priests into their home. One Jesuit became their chaplain and built upon the spiritual foundation that Róża's mother had laid. Fr. Kiejnowski is

---

[5]*Life*, Ch. I.
[6] Julia Stanisława Bakalarz, O.P., *Contemplation and Action in Mother Kolumba Białecka's Spiritual Life*, WAM, Kraków, 1994, 11.

A very young Róża

Her mother Anna Ernestyna

Her father Franciszek

credited with instilling in Róża her deep and life-shaping love of the Blessed Sacrament. He also arranged for her to meet a similar soul, a girl who later became Sister Innocenta in the Congregation of the Blessed Sacrament. Her and Róża's friendship, fed on a common love of Christ, lasted throughout their lives.

Another important religious influence were the Dominicans in the Białeckis' parish, Podkamień. They celebrated the sacraments for the Białecki family and were very involved in their lives. Their parish also had an impact on Róża, since it boasted a statue of Our Lady which was associated with hundreds of miracles and the destination of many pilgrims. For her part, Róża recognized as an adult that her love of the Virgin Mary drew her to Christ from a young age.

This stood out in two particular moments. Róża was allowed to receive her First Holy Communion at the unusually-young age of

Róża's younger sister, nicknamed Władzia (left), and her older sister Maria (bottom) were the only other surviving Białecki children, but both would precede Róża in death.

eight[7], on the feast of Our Lady's Immaculate Conception. She fell seriously sick beforehand, probably from her first attack of tuberculosis, so the chaplain celebrated Mass the evening before, and in the early morning brought Holy Communion to Róża's bedside.

Years later, Róża described this "first encounter with You, [Christ]" as being the event that "number[ed] me among Her [Mary's] children."[8] Our Lady's intercession was inseparably linked with Christ in her mind.

The eleven-year-old's Confirmation, in 1850, also closely connected the Blessed Virgin with her future. After receiving the Holy Spirit's gifts in the sacrament, Róża made a promise before the miraculous Marian image in Podkamień. She vowed that she would give herself to serve God, totally, in a religious order.

---

[7] Pope Pius X (1903-14) had not yet encouraged the reception of Holy Communion by children, so the fact that Róża received the Eucharist before her early teens was a testament to her mature understanding of the faith.

[8] *Spiritual Inspirations*, Dec. 7, 1873.

Podkamién's miraculous image of Our Lady, dating perhaps to the 1700s, was a pilgrimage destination.

Remains of the Podkamién parish on "Rosary Mountain." Dominican friars were martyred or driven from this site time and again since first establishing a mission there in the 1200s.

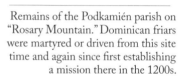

Although unaware of this vow, Róża's parents provided her with some firsthand experience with religious when they sent her and Władzia to a boarding school run by the Sisters of Sacré Coeur in Lvov. Róża was already fifteen, so she was nearing the end of her formal education. She only stayed with the Sisters of Sacré Coeur for about two years, but those years were certainly formative. The boarding school was highly reputed for its academics, especially in the humanities, and Róża showed herself to be a sharp student.[9]

Classmates recalled Róża to be a serious girl whose maturity influenced their own behavior. She was known to prefer spending time in the chapel, oblivious to the reputation for "goodness" and authenticity that she was establishing. During these years, she fed her

[9] Zygmunt Mazur, O.P., and Joachim Roman Bar, OFMConv., *Faithful to Hidden Love*, Publishing House of the Discalced Carmelites, Kraków, 1989, 14.

love of prayer by joining several devotional groups: the Association of the Angels, the Association of Mary's Children, and a confraternity of the Holy Rosary run by the Dominicans. Taken all together, these may seem excessive, but they were certainly no passing fancy. They included devotions that characterized Róża's spiritual life until the day she died—her secretary Sr. Benwenuta noted how much she treasured the medal marking her membership with Mary's Children, "with which she died. It appeared an obvious intention of the Lord Jesus that Mother [Kolumba] should serve Him in the Order devoted to honoring His Immaculate Mother."[10]

But Róża did not join the community which seemed most obvious, the Sisters of Sacré Coeur. Nor did she, after leaving their school, seem to have much direction as to where she was called. She did finally break the news to her parents that she was intent on religious life, and met with an obstacle in the form of her father. Not that he was opposed in principle to having a daughter become a nun; he did not want to curb her religious practices, nor did he want to force her to marry. Franciszek Białecki just could not imagine parting with his most beloved daughter.

While characteristically obedient to her father, Róża could not forget her vocation. Things came to a head when Róża's tuberculosis hit and she failed to respond to treatment. She appeared to be "fading away…severely ill, even though not bedridden," and doctors estimated that she may live three more months – at best.[11] More than the tuberculosis, it became clear that Róża's call to the convent weighed upon her. Franciszek did everything in his power to try to ensure Róża's life, including giving alms and having Masses said, but

---

[10] *Life*, Ch. XXIV.
[11] *Life*, Ch. II.

he could not bring himself to give Róża his consent. Finally, a Jesuit friend intervened with the suggestion: if Franciszek let Róża enter a convent, at least she would die happy and he would not have a guilty conscience after her death. And perhaps the Lord would reward his sacrifice by restoring Róża's health.

This last idea was the clincher. The possibility that Róża might survive made Franciszek resolve that she could enter a convent— "even one abroad"—if only God allowed Róża her health.[12] He commissioned the priest to break the news to Róża, and upon receiving it, Róża immediately began to improve. But never again was the topic broached between them: Róża's father himself died very soon after, in February 1855.

Róża was only sixteen that winter, yet her tiny size—which remained strikingly small even as an adult—contained an unusual maturity. She became a mainstay for her heartbroken mother and younger sister (her oldest sister lived elsewhere, having already married). She comforted her family and even helped her mother arrange financial affairs. Still, her call to religious life was not forgotten.

Her spiritual director of the time, a Dominican priest, suggested that Róża visit cloistered[13] Dominican nuns in Gródek, Kraków. Their Eucharist-centered life spoke strongly to Róża, and her visit would be the first step towards entry. So Róża eagerly made plans to travel to Gródek. For the time being, Mrs. Białecka stayed with ill Władzia in Lvov, and sent Róża to spend the summer with her older sister in their hometown near Podkamień.

---

[12] *Life*, Ch. II.

[13] Religious women who lead hidden lives within their convent boundaries, also called "nuns" or sometimes "contemplatives". "Apostolic" or "active" religious sisters, in contrast to nuns, may frequently minister outside of their convent. "Contemplative-active" congregations combine an emphasis on prayer with active ministry.

Meanwhile, the highest superior of the Dominican friars, Master General Father Vincent Jandel, had come from Rome visit priories in Galicia. Fr. Jandel was working to reform the Order to be more observant of its Rule; he was also known for being a saintly man. Róża's spiritual director suggested that she meet him while he was visiting the friars in Podkamień. Róża agreed to the meeting, intending to tell Fr. Jandel of her vocational discernment and to receive any decision from him as though it came from God. Terrible rain, all night long, might have deterred anyone else from braving the muddy roads, but Róża showed up at the priory, fully resolute.[14]

This meeting with Fr. Jandel was life-changing. The Master General made it clear to Róża that she should not become a nun in Gródek—not only was the life there in need of reform, but he perceived that Róża had apostolic interests not to be confined to the cloister. She wanted to bring Christian education to her countrymen living in poverty; Fr. Jandel wanted to revive[15] the contemplative-

---

Active sisters have only sporadically had official recognition within the Catholic Church; during some centuries, their official status was much the same as that of groups of lay people or they were required to be cloistered. Until the late 20th century, active Dominican sisters and laity were both called "Third Order" while nuns were distinguished as "Second Order."

[14] Cf. Bl. Hyacinthe-Marie Cormier, O.P., *Life of Alexandre-Vincent Jandel, O.P.: Seventy-Third Master General of the Friars Preachers*, trans. George G. Christian, O.P., and Richard L. Christian (New Priory Press: 2015), 339.

[15] Religious congregations had been greatly reduced under Austrio-Hungarian reforms, especially during the reign of Joseph II (1765-1790). The emperor closed two-thirds of convents and monasteries (over 1200 in all) or forced them to take on active ministries. Although he targeted contemplative orders, regarding them as "useless", many active congregations were eradicated as well (Eduard Habsburg, "They Did Nothing But Pray", *First Things*, Web, 27 June 2019. See also "The question of utility: The 'Klostersturm' under Joseph II," *The World of the Habsburgs*, Web, 2020). The impact on the Dominicans specifically is unclear, but the Order that traced its presence in Poland back to St. Dominic's day was certainly reduced. Some Dominican friars were overloaded by Mass commitments but so poor that they had take on work in the post office (Mazur, 28). The Third Orders—as they were often considered on par with confraternities—were likely suppressed altogether and it seems that the nuns in Gródek were the only Dominican women remaining in Poland by Róża's day.

Alexandre- Vincent Jandel was Master General of the Order of Preachers (Dominicans).

active Dominican sisters in Poland. Their aims coincided well.

Fr. Jandel advised Róża to enter a new convent of Regular[16] Dominican Sisters of the Third Order in Nancy, France. There she would experience active Dominican life as well as be formed as a sister. After some time, he hoped, she could return to Poland to start her own foundation—a new congregation of Third Order Dominican sisters. Although Róża was yet seventeen, unambitious and hugely inexperienced in the ways of the world, Fr. Jandel thought her capable of becoming a foundress. He later described what he had perceived

---

[16] Meaning those who follow the established Rule of the Order; St. Dominic's brethren chose to follow the Rule of St. Augustine, supplemented by their Constitutions and Customs.

Just before leaving for Nancy, Róża agreed to have her photo taken for her mother's sake. She was already in her traveling clothes.

that gave him such an idea: "A pure heart, sensitive to the interests of God, a mind as frank as it was honest, a flame of zeal all the more persevering the more it was contained…." [17]

In Fr. Jandel, Róża perceived not only a holy man, but a very fatherly one as well. He cared about her realizing her vocation with all of her God-given talents. But he worried that it would be hard for her to leave her country and family indefinitely—"I know to what degree Polish people are attached to their country," he said. "… So, consider whether you possess ample strength and generosity to give to our Lord a complete and unlimited sacrifice of [your] country and your family and make vows in these circumstances, with no conditions and without looking back!" Róża could never have anticipated such an outcome to their conversation, but she "was delighted…and gave everything as a sacrifice." [18] As she'd resolved, she accepted the Master General's suggestion as though it came from God Himself. While her sister resignedly wept, Róża felt a sense of deep peace.

Róża's great trust in the Master General was an extension of her trust in her Heavenly Father. And both would prove worthy of her trust. In tough times as well as triumphant, Fr. Jandel would support Róża with fatherly letters, advice, and encouragement for as long as he lived. Her own father, Franciszek Białecki, had made a great sacrifice in giving Róża permission to leave home and family. Now, Fr. Jandel took the place of Róża's father on earth, helping her to carry on her father's spirit of sacrifice and realize her vow by entering a convent— "even one abroad."

---

[17] Cormier, 338.

[18] *Life*, Ch. II.

{ Chapter 2 }
PURSUING GOD'S PLAN

A major piece had fallen into place: a plan for Róża to realize her religious vocation while also educate the poor and needy. But, as she set off for Nancy, France, in May 1857, Róża must have expected difficulties to founding a brand-new congregation.

The first difficulty, as Fr. Jandel had anticipated, was homesickness. It hit hard. No other sister in Nancy knew Polish, and Róża pined to hear a single word of her native language. She was assigned to assist in the sacristy, which gave her extra opportunities to be near the Blessed Sacrament, but the chapel also became a site for tears, as Róża fled behind the altar to read letters from home. She recalled "imploring the Hidden Savior to give me strength to fight that tormenting suffering. Oh, if not for the great mercy of the Lord, I do not know if I would have survived. ... Each time that I was tormented by my longing, I would run to our Mistress. Mother Mistress would always comfort me by saying that everything would pass."[19] But one day, the Mistress shocked Róża by saying: "My child, you have no vocation, you have to

---

[19] *Life*, Ch. II.

Above: the convent cloister in Nancy, France.

return to your country and your family because you will not be a nun."
Róża was so terrified at the thought of losing her vocation that her
homesickness disappeared, afterwards only to momentarily return. It
was as though "by divine inspiration" that "this good Mother cured me
with her words," she later said.[20]

Father Jandel had suggested the Nancy Dominicans on purpose:
Dominicans had recently founded this convent of the Third Order
to enjoy restored religious freedoms in France and take their part in
educating society. Here, Róża could absorb the Dominican spirituality,
see how it functioned in an active community, and understand the
revival which Fr. Jandel desired. She was also able to meet influential
Dominican priests of the time: Fr. Dominic Lacordaire, a famous
orator who had reinstated the Dominicans in France, and his saintly
comrade-in-arms Fr. Hyacinth Besson, who was also an artist. Her
stay in Nancy gave Róża the opportunity to observe Dominican life
even as she was formed by it, and the sisters there were very kind to her.

[20] *Life*, Ch. II.

Nancy foundress and novice mistress, Mother of St. Rose Lejeune.

They welcomed her with great warmth and took thoughtful care for her health. Mother of St. Rose Lejeune, who was foundress, prioress, and novice mistress, kept loving and supportive correspondence with Róża until the day of her death. She warmly greeted news of the "new sprig" of Dominican sisters which Róża was to found.

In this setting, Róża became a novice, receiving the Dominican habit and the name "Sister Maria Kolumba" in April 1858. Like all her sisters after her, Maria Kolumba would receive her first name in honor of the Mother of God. The second, Kolumba, is Latin for "dove" and must have seemed fitting for this pale, docile, and diminutive Pole. In her descriptions of Róża, Mother of St. Rose Lejeune seemed especially taken by her "tiny" size and "angelic" disposition.[21]

Sister Kolumba's vocation was not clear sailing from this point on, however; she continued to grapple with a desire to enter a cloistered convent. But in his unfailing letters, Fr. Jandel convinced her that her

---

[21] Serafina Steinig, O.P., *Mother Maria Kolumba Białecki: Foundress of Polish Dominican Sisters,* 1838-1887, Trans. Maria Ferensowicz. Century Publishing, Toronto, 1983, 79.

love would not allow her to stay behind the grille and her virtues would be best developed in the contemplative-active life. The cloistered convent in Kraków, of which she dreamt, was not for her, "either for your health or your soul"[22].

Because Fr. Jandel knew that Sister Kolumba was outside his authority (she was subject to her Mother Superiors in Nancy, not to the Master General), or to completely sever her attachments, Fr. Jandel also warned her that he could not promise she would ever return to Poland. He wrote to Sister Kolumba that she must make a total sacrifice of home and country, and prepare herself to stay in France for the rest of her life.

With such resolutions, Sister Kolumba made her first, temporary, profession of vows in April 1859. It seemed that she might stay in Nancy forever —until Mrs. Białecka herself stepped in to ask for Sister Kolumba's return to Poland. Mrs. Białecka thought that Sister Kolumba's return might help the family finances; but she also was eager to jumpstart the new congregation of Dominicans.[23] Yet, while Sister Kolumba's superiors gave her their blessing to go and begin a new foundation, not a single sister left Nancy to assist her. However nerve-wracking it may have been to set out alone, Sister Kolumba returned to Poland in June and joined her mother in Lvov.

At twenty years old[24], Sister Kolumba was legally still a minor, so her mother's support was essential for approaching the Polish authorities with the plan. Providentially, Mrs. Białecka was an enthusiastic supporter of this mission, having begun the revival of lay Dominicans by professing vows herself some years before.[25] And the first authority

---

[22] *Life*, Ch. III.

[23] *Life*, Ch. III.

[24] See note 2, on p. iv.

[25] *Life*, Ch. I.

Bishop Antoni Józef Manastyrski
was the first to bless Sister
Kolumba's initiative.

they approached, Bishop Manastyrski of Lvov, responded with kindness and encouragement. He advised Sister Kolumba to begin by translating the constitutions of the Nancy Dominicans into Polish, while staying in a convent in Lvov.

But God arranged that Sister Kolumba had to move to Przemyśl. Benedictine sisters in that town gave her residence when no convent in Lvov was willing. People had begun to make malicious comments about Sister Kolumba;[26] while the exact content has not been recorded, we can imagine from where some of it stemmed. This spanking-new sister had grand pretensions of becoming a Mother Superior. She had just returned from a foreign country with novel ideas of religious life, and had no intentions of remaining behind a cloister grille. Just who did she think she was?

Besides paining Sister Kolumba, such talk must have caused her to question how realistic her plans were. She decided to be patient but pragmatic: she would stay in Przemyśl some months beyond

---

[26] cf. Steinig, 13.

those required to translate the constitutions and statutes, but if no opportunity materialized, she would return to Nancy forever.

Prayers and Providence came through. Founding a Third Order community was, after all, not Róża Białecka's plan, but up to God. In April 1860, her seventh month in Przemyśl, Sister Kolumba received a visitor who was very interested in a foundation of Dominican sisters. Fr. Julian Leszczyński was a priest who had daydreamed about active Dominican sisters as a young boy, even though there were none in Poland at the time. In junior high school, he had gone so far as to draw convents of active Dominicans and give names to the sketched sisters! He had worked in two parishes already, but found them unsuitable for realizing his dream of partnering with sisters. In 1860, he had just received the appointment of pastor in Wielowieś—an appointment which depended on the local nobility, who immediately were impressed by and supportive of Fr. Leszczyński. This gave him a great deal of stability and freedom in his role as pastor; now, he was eager to learn more about the possibility of bringing Dominican sisters to his parish. And everything he heard from Sister Kolumba pleased him. It seemed that Providence had brought them together.

Sister Kolumba left the meeting full of happiness and gratitude, which she immediately presented to the Lord in the Blessed Sacrament. Anticipating that her troubles were not yet over, she lay prostrate and "sacrificed herself in a spirit of gratitude to the Lord, ready to accept all crosses and suffering which might await her in the work of the Foundation."[27] She, her mother, and Fr. Leszczyński immediately began putting things into place to establish a convent in Wielowieś.

The first few steps met with mostly blessings. The bishop over Wielowieś, Bishop Wierzchlejski of Przemyśl, accepted and

---

[27] *Life*, Ch. IV.

Father Julian Leszczyński was eager to have Dominican sisters work in his parish.

Bishop Adam Jasiński of the Przemyśl diocese gave unfailing support to the new Congregation.

encouraged Sister Kolumba's proposal, but he was soon moved to be Archbishop of Lvov. Undaunted, Sister Kolumba presented the plans to his successor as well, and was fortunate to find a kindly heart in Bishop Jasiński. He advised her to begin Dominican life in Wielowieś under the supervision of Fr. Leszczyński—and even quietly open a novitiate—without waiting for further approval. The community could put the translated constitutions to the test before seeking official approval from the bishop and the civil government.

Fr. Leszczyński, on his part, began cultivating support from the Wielowieś locals and neighboring clergy. Sister Kolumba and Mrs. Białecka visited in September and met with warm reception. The countess Gabryela Tarnowska and her son, who owned Wielowieś, promised their support. They offered property across from the church as site for a convent, as well as construction materials from the forests. In the meantime, Fr. Leszczyński set about converting a wooden school building to serve as a temporary convent.

Another key element, for which Sister Kolumba certainly prayed, was good candidates to become her first sisters. Already, four had stepped forward, including one who was a longtime servant in the Białecki family. She, Katarzyna Murzynska, would be the first "converse" sister.[28] By allowing for converse sisters in the Congregation, Mother Kolumba included women whose lack of education, social standing, or aptitude might have otherwise kept them from a religious vocation. As Mother later stated, even the customarily required dowry

---

[28] Sometimes called "second choir" as opposed to "first choir" sisters, converse sisters did more manual labor in the community without being held to the same prayer obligations or apostolic work, such as chanting the Divine Office or teaching catechesis. This distinction ended after the Second Vatican Council (1962-5).

The young foundress, Mother Kolumba Białecka.

could be dispensed with if circumstances demanded.[29]

So it was that, with good prospects in hand, Sister Kolumba returned briefly to Nancy to make her perpetual profession of vows on April 1, 1861. While there, the 22-year-old also received from her superiors the necessary authority to begin her foundation in Poland. During her trip, she stopped by Kraków to visit the owner of Wielowieś, Countess Tarnowska, who later described her impression of Sister Kolumba: "It is difficult to live up to one's own name more than she," she said. "A real dove; white on the inside and outside, and the dark blueness of the sky is reflected and treasures revealed in the depth of her eyes." Not only did Sister Kolumba's religious name suit her, but she seemed to be blessed with a knack for winning the esteem of crucial patrons.

At some point during these preparations, Sister Kolumba received a different and more promising offer: solid buildings in Warez that could sooner serve as a convent and were closer to her family. Although Wielowieś' prospects were significantly less and largely hypothetical, Sister Kolumba chose the "malarial, out-of-the-way village"[30] over the much more attractive possibilities in Warez. "In spite of her young age and lack of experience," she had the wise sense that, "in order to work well for the people, one needs to live with them, sharing their hardships and fate."[31] So it was that, with two candidate sisters in tow, Mother Kolumba moved to Wielowieś on May 30, 1861.

---

[29] Letter to Mother Marcelina Darowska of June 6, 1881; in which the dowry is called an "application of several hundred florins."

[30] Mazur, 20.

[31] Mazur, 20.

{ Chapter 3 }
REVOLUTIONARY
ACTION

When Mother Kolumba showed up in Wielowieś with plans to "educate the peasants," the local gentry were guarded. Just fifteen years ago, in 1846, peasants of the area had been incited into a bloody revolt and had murdered between one and two thousand nobles and their officials. They had destroyed about ninety percent, or at least 470, of the manor houses in the Tarnow region.[32] Tarnow was barely 60 miles from Wielowieś, so this slaughter was undoubtedly still fresh in the nobles' minds.

Serfdom had been an establishment in Poland for more than three centuries. From the early 1500s, peasants were obliged by law to work for their landowner for one day a week…at minimum. Eventually in 1848—spurred by the 1846 uprising and probably to hamstring the Polish opposition—the Austrian government abolished serfdom in Galicia. But the centuries had left their mark. Besides a widespread belief that the peasants were genetically, spiritually, and physically inferior, serfdom had encouraged a lack of work ethic. Serfs were

---

[32] "Galician Slaughter," Wikipedia, 11 June 2020. Web.

inclined to show up late, use poor tools, and work slowly for their lords; now many of the freed peasants enjoyed the only comfort they knew: inactivity.[33]

With their labor freed and hard to hire, the nobles weren't likely to welcome someone bearing Marx-like ideas of empowering the masses. As she began paying calls around Wielowieś, Mother Kolumba certainly walked into some hostile drawing rooms, and it's a testament to her diplomacy that she was able to win over the nobility. Indeed, "[s]ome of the gentlemen among the citizens who were against the convent changed their minds after only one conversation with Mother Kolumba, concluding that the convent established by her would be a useful institution and that she was an extraordinary creature, this Mother Kolumba!"[34]

We don't know the exact content of these conversations, but we can imagine Mother Kolumba's part went something like this: "Let me teach these peasants the love of the Father, from which comes true love of fatherland. Let me teach them about the Son of God who became one of them and worked diligently with his own hands. Let me teach them the Spirit of Christ, which alone promises peace."

Perhaps the lessons of Róża's parents were voiced in these words. Franciszek and Anna Ernestyna were both known for their humane attitude towards the peasants, and for providing resources to those hit by poverty or hardship. Foreseeing its benefits in uniting the peasants for Poland, Róża's father had joined with other landowners to ask for the abolition of serfdom as early as 1843—a petition that the government had ignored, seeing it as inconvenient to Austria's aims.[35]

---

[33] Waldemar Kuligowski, "A history of Polish serfdom: Theses and antitheses," Eurozine, Web, 13 Feb. 2018.

[34] *Life*, Ch. IV.

[35] Mazur, 10.

So Franciszek Białecki enacted his own reforms and freed the serfs on his land. In hindsight, the 1846 uprising showed Franciszek Białecki's actions to be both prescient and charitable.

As a child, Róża had absorbed her parents' charity and taken it even further, interceding for specific kindnesses or forgiveness for a peasant. She had shown unusual understanding for the household servants, tried to lighten their work, and even spoke up to justify them to her parents—all of which won her their grateful love and the nickname "Angel".

This "Angel" was now intent on bringing the Good News to the peasants, not social revolution. Her goal was simple, and far from that of her rabble-rousing contemporary, Karl Marx. She was driven by the same compassion and love of truth that had moved her Order's founder, St. Dominic, to leave his quiet life as a canon and preach the Gospel. Mother Kolumba was convinced that real catechesis would improve the lives of the peasants as well as the society as a whole—but ultimately, she was focused on their quality of eternal life. As Mother defined it, the sisters had "no other aim than…to spread the Kingdom of God in souls."[36]

But in different ways, Mother's actions *were* revolutionary. This daughter of the Polish gentry wasn't afraid to be found serving members of the lowest class. Within five days of arriving in Wielowieś, Mother paid her first visit to a sick peasant. Mother Kolumba rolled up her sleeves and nursed the peasants, watched over their children, and was even known to clean their homes. When she couldn't do it herself, she sent her sisters. With a congregation in the bud and a harvest at the ready, Mother Kolumba didn't have the luxury of keeping her novices

---

[36] *Directory for the Novitiate*, also quoted in the Constitutions of the Sisters of St. Dominic, Ch. 1.

at home for sheltered formation. Like St. Dominic, she couldn't wait for her sisters to be many or masterful before she sent them into the field. So, before social workers were a thing or Florence Nightingale blazed the way, the Sisters of St. Dominic were deep at work on the home front.

In fact, within one year of their arrival, a revolution did lead the local Poles to take up arms. Their unsuccessful battles resulted in many fallen men, so the sisters turned their attention to the injured. Mother organized a field hospital in Wielowieś and then traveled to another town, Dzikow, to personally help in a hospital there. Eleven years later, in 1873, danger still more directly attacked, in the form of a cholera epidemic. The sisters poured themselves into care for cholera victims, even though it exposed their own sisters to danger and cost one postulant's precious life.

Mother hadn't studied psychology or pedagogy, but she intuited something basic to both: you can't teach the spirit or intellect until physical needs are addressed. Caring for wounded soldiers wasn't to fulfill a political agenda but the Gospel mandate of charity. Similarly, cleaning a woman's home allowed the resident some desperately needed rest, while tending the sick gave their family members a chance to work in the fields. Mother's instructions to novices revealed her driving motive: "Through service offered to the body, you can easily influence the soul of the poor sick [people] and turn them to the Dearest Creator."[37] Tackling basic needs was both a prerequisite and

---

[37] *Directory for the Novitiate*, 140. See also Bakalarz, 66: "According to Mother Białecka, care for the sick constitutes a wider religious action. By fulfilling deeds of mercy recommended by Christ, you establish contact with people, get to know their daily life and hardships, [and] help them live in a way worthy of God's child[ren]." Care for the sick also provides opportunity to teach the meaning of suffering and prevent it from being wasted. As Mother urged a sick sister, "Each moment of suffering is important, especially when life may end soon" (Letter to Sisters in Wielkie Oczy, Feb. 18, [1874]).

opportunity for establishing human dignity and social stability—all of which prepared the way for religious education.

In this way, Mother went beyond the traditional apostolate of the Dominican friars, who focused on study and preaching, and of the nuns, who supported the friars' ministry through prayer and penance. Mother's unusual congregation aroused prejudice and even hostility.[38] Yet her actions were right in line with those of Dominicans saints such as Catherine of Siena and Rose of Lima. They had each joined the Third Order—though not convents—and were famous for tending the sick. Like them, Mother imitated Christ's example in preaching the Gospel. Before Jesus ever commissioned his disciples to "teach them to observe all that I have commanded you,"[39] he sent them to prepare the way by healing the sick, cleansing lepers, and casting out demons.[40] Jesus illustrated what Mother intuited: people will be much more receptive to the Gospel when they see its fruit, witnessing true compassion for physical and psychological needs.

Mother showed similar compassion in her educational outreach. In mid-August, the sisters officially began teaching in the parish school, but the peasants usually limited their children's schooling to six years total and, of those, only the winter months.[41] So Mother taught her sisters to seek out their students wherever they were, even if that meant chasing them down in the pastures for on-the-spot lessons.

The trailblazing didn't stop there. Because most women religious were cloistered, they were limited to educating girls (to whom they could also offer room and board). They weren't about to take responsibility for the peasant boys of obscure villages. But Mother wrote a letter to

---

[38] Mazur, 21.

[39] Matthew 28:20.

[40] Matthew 10:8.

[41] Mazur, 24.

the archbishop asking for permission to run co-ed schools.[42] In her letter, she argued that if the sisters could not teach boys as well, the boys would be deprived of knowledge. She believed that education would make a substantial difference in their lives. Once granted the permission, the sisters added classes targeting practical skills that the boys would need, paralleling their classes for girls' manual skills.

The sisters were no less intentional in admitting Jewish and Eastern Orthodox students to their schools. Their desire to teach Gospel values to all types of youth notably decreased the local tensions and conflicts in these out-of-the-way villages where "peoples' worldviews [were] outdated at least half a century," and Jews largely disliked Christians.[43] One letter from villagers recorded that "God-oriented thoughts …which [the sisters] instilled" caused domestic peace to prevail, demoralizing behavior to decrease, and unity to "now dominate among our inhabitants."[44] Villagers recognized that the sisters' influence on their daughters alone promised positive effects on their future children, husbands, and citizenry.[45] When such education was extended to the boys and children of other religions as well, the effects on society were even faster and more direct.

Besides reaching out to all types of children, Fr. Leszczyński encouraged the sisters to broaden their religion programs to include older youth and adults. He also entrusted them with preparing children to receive the sacraments for the first time—a responsibility

---

[42] Bakalarz, 91.

[43] Bakalarz, 92.

[44] Letter of July 4, 1882 quoted in Bakalarz, p. 90-91, n. 558.

[45] Bakalarz, 92. As one villager from Wielkie Oczy attested in a letter, "During only eight months since [the sisters] took over the school…the youth have changed physically and morally beyond recognition. They make extraordinary progress in learning and in female manual skills—which had been so neglected and abandoned" (quoted in Bakalarz, 91-2).

usually reserved to the clergy.[46] Regular Sunday catechesis would not become common in Poland until almost two decades later.[47] But the sisters conducted such programs with vigor. On Sundays, they would disperse to various villages for adult and youth catechesis.

Within their carefully planned programs, the topics ranged from religion to agriculture as the sisters tried to address the peasants' various needs. They purposefully taught both vocal and mental prayers. At a time when Catholics did not generally read the Bible on their own[48], the sisters shared the Gospel and guided meditation on Scripture.[49] Predating modern youth groups, they organized many spiritual associations and led recreational meetings. Above all, the sisters focused on the liturgy, supplementing the Sunday readings with time-honored homilies and hymns. Villagers would then join singing in procession with a cross back to Wielowieś to participate in Vespers. These Sunday activities intentionally kept the peasants from patronizing the tavern, changing their life habits for the better.[50]

Thus Mother headed up an unstinting apostolate of catechesis, education, and care for the sick and needy. She had a hand in all of it herself, from stopping in to quiz and praise her sisters' pupils (when

---

[46] Steinig, 15.

[47] Bakalarz, 65.

[48] Due to the many and divisive factions that came from private interpretations of Scripture, the Council of Trent (1545-63) stressed caution in reading Scripture on one's own, especially from dubious translations. But Scripture itself was always considered crucial to the life of faith, and soon after Mother Kolumba's time, Pope Pius X (1903-14) would commend the society of St. Jerome for encouraging the faithful to read and meditate on the Gospels (cited by Pius XII in *Divino Afflante Spiritu*, 1943, sec. 9). As the Second Vatican Council (1962-5) affirmed: the Church "forcefully and specifically exhorts all the Christian faithful...to learn 'the surpassing knowledge of Jesus Christ' (Phil. 3:8) by frequent reading of the divine Scriptures" (*Dei Verbum*, 1965, sec. 25, quoted also in *The Catechism of the Catholic Church*, para. 133). For detailed discussions of the Council of Trent, see Robert McNally, S.J., "The Council of Trent and Vernacular Bibles," Web, (n.d.), esp. 226-7.

[49] Bakalarz, 90.

[50] Steinig, 17.

she wasn't teaching classes herself), to leading the parish choir, to directing donations to just the person in need. The sisters were known to help all those who came to their door, whether it be for clothing, healthcare, or advice. The "Reverend Maids", as the villagers called them, were often summoned to attend the dying, many of whom expressed a desire "only for a sister to pray beside them during their agony and to not leave them until their last breath."[51] Throughout their last days, the sisters prepared the dying spiritually, arranged for them to receive the Anointing of the Sick, and were rewarded by witnessing many calm and holy deaths. The sisters also made a habit of attending funerals in the parish. All was done to preach the Gospel through their way of life.

The sisters' success, socially as well as catechetically, may best be expressed by the words of one peasant, Józef Klimek. Seven years after their arrival in Wielowieś, the governor asked him about the sisters' influence, and Józef praised their devotion to the sick. But first and foremost, he claimed, "We and our wives are only stepfathers and stepmothers; the 'Reverend Maids' are true mothers to our children because they teach them to know and love our Lord!"[52]

---

[51] *Life,* Ch. VI.
[52] *Life,* Ch. VIII.

Chapter 4
THE CONTEMPLATIVE
SIDE OF LIFE

Amid all of this action—or rather, to fuel it—Mother Kolumba held to the Dominican principle of contemplation. The motto "to contemplate and to hand on to others the fruit of one's contemplation"[53] underlay the lifestyle outlined by the Congregation's constitutions. Mother Kolumba emphasized that the sisters' primary purpose was not to teach, catechize, or nurse the needy, but to proclaim the truth of the Gospel by their lives. According to Mother's reasoning, the testimony of the sisters' lives would speak as much as—or more than—their words, so they must live the truth. To do that, they must first know the Truth, beginning with a strong faith and cultivating it through contemplation.

Mother Kolumba stressed the sisters' obligation to be well formed themselves before ministering to others. She instructed novices to "devote yourself passionately to education," for the service of God's glory and "to become more useful to our neighbors in the future."[54] In this she echoed the very first constitutions of the Dominican friars,

---

[53] *Contemplare et contemplata aliis tradere,* long a Dominican motto.

[54] *Directory for the Novitiate,* 140-1 and 64, also connected to St. Dominic's maxim as quoted in the "Ratio Formationis," see below.

which stated that the labor of study was intended "to make us capable of being useful to the soul of our neighbor."[55] For her part, Mother Kolumba regretted that women of her time did not receive more theological instruction, but she strove to pass on a firm grasp of the faith as well as of religious life and Dominican spirituality. She sought formation through wise reading and spiritual direction, and made spiritual reading a regular practice for her sisters—"To study always"[56] was another Dominican cornerstone that underlay her foundation.[57] "Study hard," Mother wrote to the novices, describing this as both a luxury and a duty in their life.[58] Even though the Congregation was strapped for money, it put orders in at the publishing house (some of which were for books to give to the peasants, to spread "the reading habit"[59]). In this way, too, the sisters imitated their Dominican forefathers, who—despite their poverty in all other respects—had kept valuable books, considering them indispensable to their ministry.

While Mother intended that her sisters be well educated to carry out their ministries, no candidate was turned away because of a lack of education.[60] The demand for professionally prepared sisters easily exceeded their availability, so that some sisters learned from more experienced ones on the job. But such were temporary stopgaps; the sisters generally valued professional training.[61] In this, Mother

---

[55] Prologue of the Constitutions of the Order of Preachers of 1220, as quoted in Guy Bedouelle, O.P., Saint Dominic: The Grace of the Word, Ignatius Press, 1987, 159.

[56] *Semper studere.*

[57] See "Ratio Formationis," Part III: Permanent Formation, V. Fields Related to Perpetual Formation, 5. Doctrinal, intellectual, and professional formation.

[58] Letter to Sr. Alberta and Novice and Converse Sisters (n.d.).

[59] Bakalarz, 92.

[60] Bakalarz, 94.

[61] See Bakalarz, 94, and her reference to the use of medical literature, teacher training courses and certificates, and an emphasis on "the quality and qualifications of sisters who would work as teachers" in the early days of the Congregation.

Kolumba anticipated Pope Pius XII's call for religious to be as professionally competent as their lay counterparts.

But Mother Kolumba kept in mind that spiritual formation was the most essential for a sister to live out her apostolate. To Dominicans, study is indeed a means of spiritual progress, but prayer is the surest school. Mother drew on St. Thomas Aquinas[62] to emphasize that "it is precisely this holy exercise [of prayer] which gives us the strength needed to meet all the obligations of our state in life." What is more, "Only through prayer can…we draw benefits from everything for the sake of our spiritual progress." [63]

Therefore Mother Kolumba incorporated regular prayer into the sisters' lives. "With our busy life," she wrote for prospective candidates, "we always practice around five hours or more of spiritual exercises."[64] Although a Dominican can always ask to be dispensed from an obligation which impedes the apostolate, Mother rarely excused sisters from prayers.[65] Like Fr. Jandel, she believed that fidelity to prayer was a priority for ministry.

Among their spiritual exercises, the sisters prayed the entire Divine Office,[66] (except mid-night Matins). This meant that they joined together at least four times a day[67] to recite the Psalms and other Scripture passages aloud. Sisters were also encouraged to individually

---

[62] "St. Thomas used to say that a consecrated person without prayer is like a soldier without a weapon on the day of battle," *Directory for the Novitiate*, 42.

[63] *Directory for the Novitiate*, 42, translation revised.

[64] Letter to Mother Marcelina Darowska, June 6, 1881.

[65] *Life*, Ch. XXVII.

[66] The Divine Office is an official prayer of the Church that divided the Psalms into a weekly cycle to be recited with other Scripture passages at eight times (Hours) throughout the day and night. The current form, named the Liturgy of the Hours, follows a monthly cycle of a maximum seven Hours.

[67] The time of each Hour is flexible and they may be combined so as to leave larger blocks of time available for work. For the sisters' original schedule, see *Directory for the Novitiate*, 31-38, and *Prescriptions for the Filial Houses*, 13-7.

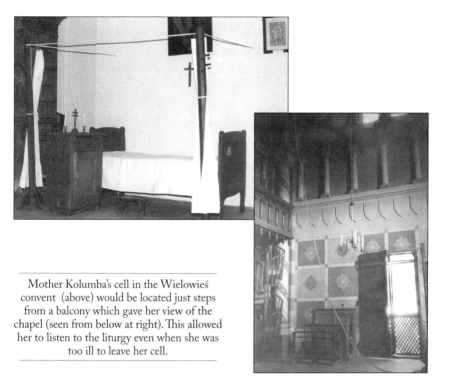

Mother Kolumba's cell in the Wielowieś
convent (above) would be located just steps
from a balcony which gave her view of the
chapel (seen from below at right). This allowed
her to listen to the liturgy even when she was
too ill to leave her cell.

and regularly reflect on Scripture, steeping themselves in the Word
of God which they preached. The rosary—which they said each day
in common if possible, privately if not—provided reflection on the
events of Christ's life, as well as an opportunity to intercede for other
souls.[68] Daily, attending Mass was a given and meditation was a must.

Despite the busyness of their lives and prayers in common,
Mother Kolumba did not forget the importance of silence to the
contemplative life. She told her sisters to love the spirit of prayer
and silence, "and you will see how the Lord will lavish graces upon
you."[69] Because of the practical need for silence to help one stay

---

[68] *Directive for the Novitiate*, 96, in which Mother Kolumba emphasizes that St. Dominic
promoted the rosary primarily for the sake of souls' conversion.
[69] *Life*, Ch. XXX.

A view from the balcony outside Mother's cell as seen today.

recollected, sisters were to keep silence in many places and at specific times throughout the day.

One silent half hour—or two—were daily devoted to meditation. Mother's description of meditation reflects the life-changing nature of prayer, in her mind: "Meditation is like a mirror, in which you ought to see yourself every day…[to] recognize your vices and a solution for their prevention. In this mirror, you should contemplate Jesus Christ's virtues in order to decorate yourself and your soul with them."[70] Extra time for such reflection was allotted in monthly days of recollection and yearly retreats. Additional prayers at certain times, various novenas, and other devotions rounded out the sisters' life—all to help them develop and live in a spirit of prayer.

Mother Kolumba personally lived what she taught. She quoted Scripture more often than any other source, revealing her frequent meditation on it.[71] She joined the common prayers as much as possible

[70] *Directory for the Novitiate*, 41, translation revised.
[71] Cf. Bakalarz, 100-1.

despite her occupations as superior and her ill health. Whereas St. Dominic was known to energetically encourage his brothers to sing louder, Mother's mere presence motivated her sisters to pray more enthusiastically.[72] She also diligently engaged in private prayer. Whether she was offering thanksgiving, pondering perplexities, or struggling with temptation, Mother would spend hours in prayer. Whatever the preoccupation of her prayer, it would leave her sisters surreptitiously staring—the love that radiated from her face amazed them.

But, Mother's secretary recorded, "compared to what she desired, she always had so little time during the day for adoration of the Blessed Sacrament."[73] So, like St. Dominic, Mother Kolumba would stay up late at night before the Blessed Sacrament. This began before the convent chapel was built, so she would take a companion across the road to the church, or ask to be locked in there alone until dawn. Eventually, these vigils were ruled out for the sake of her health[74]; but even when tuberculosis confined Mother to her room, she listened in on the community prayers from her cell above the chapel.

By this life packed with prayer and action, Mother kept accord with Dominican tradition. But she had some emphases that were as unique as they were ahead of her day. Although Mother was anxious to avoid unorthodoxy, she had a special devotion to Jesus' soul, and mused that this aspect of Christ's humanity is so rarely revered. Her meditations on Jesus' soul, in her friend's estimation, approached states of ecstasy.[75]

---

[72] *Life*, Ch. XXIII.

[73] *Life*, Ch. XXIII.

[74] *Life*, Ch. XXIII.

[75] Letter of Sr. Innocenta Tychowska to Mother Klara Borowska, March 27, 1911 (published in *Misericordias Domini in Aeternum Cantabo: Mother Kolumba Białecka at the door of eternity*, Publishing House of the Discalced Carmelites, Kraków, 2007). Actually, Sr. Innocenta concludes from Mother's description of "disappearing…in light so incomprehensible that she instantly los[t] her strength" : "Apparently, it must have been heavenly ecstasy."

Mother Kolumba predicted that, someday, a religious congregation for the adoration of Christ's soul would be founded in Poland—which indeed occurred in 1923—"But before this will happen…let us adore it now."[76] Mother encouraged sisters to say the Anima Christi[77] with especial devotion, to do their works for the sake of Christ's Soul, and to venerate this "highest Holiness" in the Eucharist.[78]

In fact, every aspect of Mother's prayer seemed to orbit around the Eucharist. Her reflections on the mysteries of faith, such as the Incarnation, Christ's Passion or Mary's intercession, all traced their way back to the Eucharist. This sacrament fed the great esteem which Mother held for the priesthood, because in the Mass Jesus subjected Himself to the words and hands of the priest. Mother Kolumba saw every virtue exemplified in the Hidden Presence in the tabernacle, such as Jesus' humility and obedience. Before making resolutions to live out such virtues as simplicity, silence, and obedience, Mother contemplated them in the Blessed Sacrament. She regarded devotion to the Eucharist as the strongest means of formation, attesting "that the Lord Jesus in Holy Communion treats me like my best mother who, with amazing love and outstanding patience, teaches a naughty child."[79] In the Eucharist, Mother Kolumba found every grace and every motivation needed amid difficulties. She reflected, "Since I communicated and united with the Lord Jesus in this way, slowly and slightly, inner transformation has been occurring in my soul…Holy Communion must have its impact, and as a result, influence[s] strongly the alteration of my thoughts, feelings, [and] will, and strengthen[s]

---

[76] Steinig, 62 and footnote. Translation modified.

[77] A traditional prayer which begins, "Soul of Christ, sanctify me…"

[78] See *Life*, Ch XXIII and Steinig, 62.

[79] *Spiritual Inspirations*, April 1882.

my will in perseverance."[80]

Because of her own personal experience, Mother Kolumba could urge sisters to turn to the Blessed Sacrament for every need. She advised them: "Sometimes it is enough to visit the Most Blessed Sacrament just once, and your inner disposition alters completely and immediately. Instead of confusion and pain, a soul is filled with peace and satisfaction. You might visit the Blessed Sacrament being weak and sad, and return full of strength, courage, and even joy."[81] "Before the Blessed Sacrament, your hearts warm up, that is what experience teaches us."[82] Mother even encouraged frequent reception of Holy Communion, which flew in the face of the times. But this anticipated the teachings of Pope Pius X, the Second Vatican Council, and Pope John Paul II, which all promoted the Eucharist as key to Christian life.

Mother felt that love of the Blessed Sacrament drew her in a particular way, and she tried to respond to this love by consciously uniting every moment and every task with the Real Presence. Whether she be walking down the hall or sitting down to eat, Mother Kolumba resolved to mentally join herself with Christ in the tabernacle. She responded to God's love in the Eucharist so ardently that her close friend described her as "an entire flaming sacrifice of exhaustion, [consumed] with love at the feet of Jesus the Host" and "a Eucharistic lamp" shining and warming the sisters' hearts with God's love.[83] This friend from childhood, Sister Innocenta, later wished that she had recorded the lifelong conversations she had had with Mother—each of them "fiery and dynamic" and always touching

---

[80] *Spiritual Inspirations*, April 1882.

[81] *Directory for the Novitiate*, Ch. XI.

[82] Letter to Sister Alana, May 4, 1874.

[83] Steinig, 80-1.

on the Blessed Sacrament. Although Sister Innocenta already belonged to a congregation dedicated to the Blessed Sacrament, she said that Mother Kolumba taught her much about adoring Christ present therein. Yet the latter still asked Sister's advice for how to live eucharistically, since Mother craved a way to "exhaust herself with love in Jesus' [Eucharistic] Presence."[84]

So strong was Mother Kolumba's love of the Eucharist that it caused her to question, more than once, whether she had mistaken her vocation. She felt drawn to the cloistered life, where she could more often engage in Eucharistic Adoration. But Mother eventually decided that she was called to live a "Eucharistic life" in a more hidden way, without the formal designation of "Sisters of the Blessed Sacrament" or the privileges given them for frequent Exposition—that is, having the consecrated Body of Christ displayed for face-to-face adoration. This was additionally difficult because not having Exposition meant that her sisters would receive Holy Communion less often than others. Characteristically, Mother found in Adoration the inspiration to "sacrifice this spiritual torment to the Lord Jesus" with the intention that her Congregation would make satisfaction for all the Eucharistic abuses that took place.[85]

Subsequently, Mother established practices of reparation for occasions when the Blessed Sacrament was insulted or neglected. She taught her sisters to frequently adore the Blessed Sacrament hidden in the tabernacle, whether it be in a group visit after each meal, on one's own throughout the day, or in extra hours of Adoration on Thursdays. On occasion, and regularly from 1883 onward, Mother did obtain permission for all-day Exposition of the Blessed Sacrament. On such

---

[84] Steinig, 80-1.

[85] *Spiritual Inspirations*, Saturday, December 7, 1873.

days, the sisters' lives revolved around Adoration; trips to town were limited and even converse sisters avoided heavy work on those days so as to be more free to pray.[86] Mother Kolumba believed that God intended her sisters to be characterized by veneration of the Blessed Sacrament. She urged her sisters to pass down the generations a love of the Eucharist so warm and deep that everyone who saw them would identify them as "'Dominicans Sisters of the Blessed Sacrament' or 'Blessed Sacrament Dominican Sisters!'"[87]

Mother Kolumba offered pointers of her own to cultivate this love of the Eucharist. In instructions to novices: "Do not ever leave the Lord Jesus before you are overwhelmed by a desire to belong to Him completely."[88] In a letter to a sister: "Oh, ask passionately, ask the Lord Jesus, with tears in your eyes, when visiting the Blessed Sacrament, to attract you more towards Him…Thank him for that need for the greatest grace, because it is like an introduction to the inner life."[89] On her deathbed: "What constitutes real happiness for a religious sister [is to] truly live with the Lord Jesus in the Mystery of the Altar; may your souls always stay there."[90] Most succinctly: "Live for Jesus, the Host."[91] This Eucharistic love was to be the foundation of the sisters' prayer, the textbook for their life, and the fuel for their apostolate.

---

[86] *Life,* Ch. XXVII.

[87] *Life,* Ch. XIX.

[88] *Directory for the Novitiate,* Ch. XI.

[89] Letter to Sister Dominika, June 1878.

[90] *Life,* Ch. XXX.

[91] Letter to Sister Dominika, June 1878, emphasis added.

Chapter 5
FORMING A RELIGIOUS FAMILY

In Mother's eyes, the Eucharist was so important to her sisters' religious life that she postponed moving into the newly-built convent until its chapel could be completed as well. This was no small decision: because funds for construction kept running out, the sisters stayed six years longer—nine years in all—in their temporary house. This housing was drafty, leaky, and almost burnt down over them! Rain dripped onto the sisters' beds so much that some would move to sleep under the dinner tables to stay dry. Yet Mother Kolumba urged the sisters not to complain about the discomforts, but to turn "a need into virtue."[92] Having left her own privileged life behind, the daughter of nobility never showed regret for the life of poverty she had chosen. Instead, Mother used circumstances and exhortations to illustrate essential

---

[92] *Life*, Ch. X. At this point a humorous anecdote deserves to be recounted: when the cold indoors was so acute that the sisters found it difficult to avoid discussing, Mother encouraged them to stop saying "Oh, it is so cold!" and to speak of something positive. This the sisters promised. Several days later, a joking sister said, "It was not too warm today," and when Mother reminded her of her promise, the smart-aleck replied: "Your Reverence, I am not saying that it is cold, I am speaking about warmth."

qualities of religious life, such as poverty, trust in God, zeal, communion with the saints, and sisterly love.

The convent under construction was to be relatively spacious and grand for the village, durable, a relief from drafts and leaks. It would allow the sisters at last to observe all the external customs of their religious life, such as prayer in choir, community meetings, and silence. But the desire for solid housing never distracted Mother Kolumba from the Congregation's purpose, which kept the poor front and center. She emphasized that the sisters' homes should always be open to the poor; that they should prioritize hospitality and no needy person should ever be turned away empty-handed. Often, the sisters collected and distributed used clothing, which Mother stressed must be in good condition—otherwise, it would be no kindness to give it away.

More than sharing with the poor, the sisters were to be characterized by sharing in others' poverty. In the words of one biographer, "Sharing destitution with the poor was a basic duty and principle Mother gave to the sisters."[93] The sisters were expected to live on a scale comparable to those they served—and they were intentionally serving in impoverished areas. In 1867, in fact, Mother Kolumba turned down an offer to establish a convent in Tarnow, because there the sisters would not be able to minister to the poor.[94]

Amid their active ministry, Mother Kolumba was sometimes sad to have very little to give—poverty pinched at the sisters themselves. But poverty did not exclude generosity, and Mother believed that the Lord would appreciate even the tiniest alms given to others. When it came

---

[93] Mazur, 31.

[94] See Mazur, 24, citing the Letter to Fr. Łobos of March 4, 1867.

to caring for the sick, she went so far as to advise, "Do not think about costs, because everything we have comes from the Lord Jesus."[95]

A sister's vow of poverty reflects precisely this: that everything belongs to God, and one depends on God for everything. Mother reinforced this practice of poverty by her own example. Close to her death, she asked the senior sisters whether they would allow her to choose some holy cards to give to dear ones, a request which brought tears to the sisters' eyes. They answered that everything in the Congregation belonged to Mother, at which she reminded them, "A nun has nothing that would belong to her."[96] A religious sister is not allowed to own or give away anything without permission, since all that God gives her is entrusted to the community.

Practicing poverty can simplify life, but it brings along its own challenges. If the sisters did not believe in God's providence, they would have had worries aplenty: along with construction costs, there were medical supplies and educational materials to buy, not to mention mouths to feed. All of which cost money the sisters didn't have. Mother Kolumba firmly believed in divine providence, but she also knew the traditional recourse of poor Dominicans: to beg. So Mother humbly sought assistance from every possible source.

Many locals contributed enthusiastically to the sisters, offering everything from brickyards to tubs of lime to buckets of grain. Some clergy actively resented the sisters' innovative involvement in the Church, but others gave stone, a large bell, and their parishioners' volunteer labor in support. Wielowieś parishioners and others carted loads of donated stone and wood. When building the convent, villagers took turn assisting the bricklayers, so that every day found 25 to 30

---

[95] *Life*, Ch. XXX.
[96] *Life*, Ch. XXVI.

volunteers on site. Their commitment remained steady no matter the season nor the demands of springtime or harvest. The same help was offered when it came to building the chapel, to which Mother Kolumba responded that the villagers should be paid this time. But they emphatically refused, arguing that, if they had refused payment to build a house for the sisters, they certainly would not accept it when building a house for Jesus Himself!

Fr. Leszczyński invested many hours at the worksite, giving input on the plans, avidly supervising, and ensuring everything was done correctly. Still, contractors and bricklayers were involved who did require payment, and over and over, funds ran out and paychecks were postponed. Mother feared that the unpaid bricklayers would quit altogether. This gave Mother Kolumba the opportunity to demonstrate—and instill in the sisters—her characteristic trust in divine providence.

Providence provided dramatically in some cases. Once, Mother's prayers were answered in the form of a horseback messenger, who knocked on the door of the temporary residence and delivered an envelope with 1000 guldens, a large sum. He left immediately, with no note in the envelope and no indication as to the benefactor's identity.

On another occasion, Fr. Leszczyński received a visitor who had already generously given 100 guldens. When he left, he discreetly deposited a donation on Father's desk. Because the visitor had already given so much, Father expected to find perhaps 10 guldens in the envelope. Instead, he found 1000! Divine providence was duly thanked for these outstanding impulses of generosity.

Still, construction was repeatedly put on pause and the project dragged on. And before Wielowieś' convent was finished, the sisters were invited to expand to another village, then another, none of which had proper housing to offer. So Mother sent out her young, barely-formed sisters (of the few she had!), two by two, on missions to collect funds from all over Poland and even Hungary. In true motherly fashion, she supported them—and the sisters in the new-sprung mission houses—through regular letters full of advice, correction, and community updates. Like St. Catherine of Siena's letters, these give much insight into Mother Kolumba's character, as well as into the traits she sought to shape in her spiritual children.

Zeal was one virtue Mother cultivated in her fledgling mendicants by repeatedly urging them to earn merits in Heaven. Mother's term, "earning merits," may seem archaic, but it reflects the timeless truth that souls in a state of grace can do actions pleasing to God and even affect the quality of their own eternal life through their responses to His grace. Mother Kolumba called this "earning merits", and she urged sisters to not waste a single chance to please God through positive acts. She imparted a sense of urgency by reflecting that, someday, every person's life would come to an end. Then too would end every sister's chance to earn merits, even if she wanted more. Mother's advice to use today to store up as many merits as possible was intended to fuel her sisters' zeal, not just in collecting alms, but in any task the day presented.[97]

While alms and gifts were attributed to God's providence, Mother encouraged gratitude to the earthly benefactors as well. Donors of property for specific houses, for example, were remembered in the sisters' prayers for perpetuity. Mother Kolumba kept her benefactors' needs in mind during their lifetimes, too. The sisters prayed zealously for one benefactor's fiancée and were commissioned to accompany

---

[97] Letter to Sr. Rajmunda and Sr. Joanna, on their collecting mission to Hungary, June 26, [1869]. See also Letter to Sr. Hyacynta on the collecting mission in Hungary [possibly 1871].

others on extended journeys for health treatments. Sisters would receive motherly instructions on just how to demonstrate thanks, such as being told to write a detailed letter to a benefactor.[98] Spiritual benefactors were also shown unflagging gratitude: Fathers Leszczyński, Vincent Jandel, and others remain in the sisters' prayers to the current day.

Heavenly benefactors were also given thanks. The Blessed Virgin and St. Joseph were gratefully regarded as spiritual parents to the Dominican Congregation, as were the forefathers Dominic, Thomas Aquinas and Hyacinth, and "Mother" Catherine of Siena. In addition, Mother often entrusted a particular cause to a particular saint, and then made pilgrimages or said novenas in thanksgiving. She would take a saint such as Teresa of Avila as patroness during a particular retreat, or entrust certain plans to Stanislaus and give prayerful thanks in the end. She also had dreams of Saints Hyacinth, Stanislaus Kostka, or Mary Magdalene appearing to her, "so she said some little prayers to each of those saints each week."[99]

Never did Mother Kolumba's spiritual relationships seem too numerous or disparate…to her, at least. Her companion Sister Benwenuta recalled when they stayed overnight at Mrs. Białecka's on one occasion, and their hostess found them up late at night. With concern, she asked why her daughter was still up so late. Sister Benwenuta replied that they had said the Liturgy of the Hours and the rosary, but now were saying the short prayers to those saints who appeared in Mother Kolumba's dreams. In reaction, Mrs. Białecka "joined her hands and said, so seriously as though she were saying a

---

[98] Letter to an unidentified sister, September 1886.
[99] *Life*, Ch. XXV.

prayer, 'Oh, saints of God, protect my beloved child but do not appear in her dreams because she will tire herself to death with these prayers.'"[100] Her point was humorous, but well-made. Still, Mother Kolumba's devotions and her accompanying gratitude seemed without limit.

This characteristic gratitude extended throughout all aspects of Mother's life and did not overlook her debt to her own mother. When visiting for what she knew would be the last time, Kolumba Białecka "fell to her mother's feet…thanking her for her motherly love and for everything."[101] Perhaps because of such natural debt to one's parents, Mother Kolumba would instruct a sister to write "a more detailed letter to [the sister's] parents…because they are very worried"[102] — and to write again in a few months.[103] She extended a sense of family from the Congregation to her own mother and even to sisters' sisters, arranging to have Masses said for them.[104]

This sense of family was deliberately cultivated within the Congregation, too, as Mother encouraged the sisters to see their superior as a real mother, and to respect priests as true fathers. Such a familial outlook was not restricted to the parent-child relationship— Mother especially stressed love between the sisters. Because a life of love imitates Jesus' life so well, Mother described love as a fourth vow binding the sisters (in addition to poverty, chastity, and obedience).[105] In this vein, she urged the older sisters to exhibit humility and

---

[100] *Life*, Ch. XXV.

[101] *Life*, Ch. XXVIII.

[102] Letter to Sisters Rajmunda and Joanna on their collecting mission in Hungary, Jan. 30, [1868].

[103] Letter to Sisters Rajmunda and Joanna on their collecting mission in Hungary, May 11, 1868.

[104] Letter to Sisters Rajmunda and Joanna on their collecting mission in Hungary, Nov. 4, [1868].

[105] *Directory for the Novitiate*, 157.

Anna Ernestyna's loving interest in the Congregation never faded. She was affectionately known as "Grandma" by all the Sisters of St. Dominic.

gentleness, and the younger sisters to submit respectfully to their elders. "I recommend to you love; unity of heart," she said just before her death: " …Remember that in love, everything can be done. Where love [is, all is] well."[106]

Mother Kolumba was not a romantic dreamer, nor blind to love's obstacles—she had her own struggles to underscore that sisterly love is not easy. At one point, Mother Kolumba identified herself to be easily tempted when "one of the sisters, especially Sister J. and P. complain to me about their difficulties…I feel how anger, my self-love rises in me, and unfortunately, I always succumb to irritation."[107] She resolved shortly thereafter: "When any of the sisters…awakens in my heart

---

[106] *Life*, Ch. XXX, translation revised.

[107] *Spiritual Inspirations*, Feast of the Seven Sorrows of the Holy Mary, 1885.

dislike and irritation—then [I will] stop the conversation or send her for something or ask her to say a prayer and to pray at the same time, to call upon God's help and grace so that I will not violate love." [108] Identifying her own weaknesses, making practical resolutions, and calling upon God's grace was a regular part of Mother Kolumba's spiritual life. She was not merely mouthing ideals when she urged her sisters to love—she could speak from personal experience about the struggles it entailed.

In her own reflections and in her instructions to sisters, Mother Kolumba melded spiritual guidelines with a practical understanding of human nature. One letter instructed two sisters to let love of Jesus and Mary rule them so as to make any bitterness, self-love, and egoism—"so much against true, fraternal and sisterly love"—disappear. [109] Mother asked rhetorically why the two seemed unable to live in harmony and unity, and beseeched them to learn about each other and the root of their disagreements. "Then," Mother Kolumba prescribed, "throw yourself at the Feet of the Crucified Savior, confess your guilt, evoke your sorrow and a strong resolution to live in a different way from now on." [110] Similarly, Mother required sisters to regularly ask each other for correction and forgiveness. To prevent petty vengefulness or proud resistance, the sister giving correction was to be motivated solely by love of the other's soul, and the one asking for correction was to be motivated by love of this love. [111]

Another letter contains a rebuke to a sister for being too quick to take offense and criticize. In straightforward terms, Mother

---

[108] *Spiritual Inspirations,* Sep. 27, 1885.

[109] Letter to Sisters Rajmunda and Ozanna on their collecting mission in Galicia, January 8, [1871].

[110] Letter to Sisters Rajmunda and Ozanna on their collecting mission in Galicia, January 8, [1871].

[111] *Directory for the Novitiate,* 115 and 117.

told the sister that she needed to invoke greater love and sisterly understanding: "Otherwise, one will turn against the other...and fault them constantly. When you live in community," Mother stated, "it is impossible to weigh every word."[112] Aware of the pitfalls of community life, Mother did everything she could to ensure virtue would flourish.

Life within the convent is no easier than life without, and may be even harder. Mother Kolumba set the bar high for her sisters, expecting them to endure hardship cheerfully, to live the life of the poor, to beg, and to never stop giving thanks. She knew the difficulties this called for, but also the strength that comes from virtue; beyond an "easy life", she knew that generosity, trust, zeal, gratitude, and sisterly love would make a religious family that could endure.

---

[112] Letter to Sister Alana in Rawa Ruska, [1886]. Translation modified for clarity.

Chapter 6
DELIGHTED TO BE DOMINICAN

Fr. Jandel was coming to Wielowieś! In 1867, eleven years after he had last seen Róża Białecka, the Master General went out of his way to visit the foundling Congregation. The convent was without a roof, the sisters lived in a simple make-shift house, and they were few in number. Because there was no railroad station nearby, Father took upon himself an uncomfortable, ten-mile carriage trip into rural Galicia. But his short stay left Fr. Jandel with a very positive impression: he could see how well Mother Kolumba had lovingly shaped her sisters, and how much she was loved by them.

His visit was combined with another momentous event, as Fr. Jandel was invited to witness the first vows of five sisters, made on October 2, 1867. After six years of careful formation, "immense" can hardly express the anticipation of this day. These were the first vows yet to be made by a Sister of St. Dominic, and the Dominican Master General accepted their profession into his hands!

Notably, Fr. Jandel's involvement in the Congregation was entirely out of fatherly interest: as Third Order Regular, the Sisters of St. Dominic were founded independently of the Order of Preachers.

But within two years, Fr. Jandel returned to Wielowieś to observe the eighth anniversary of the novitiate's opening. He celebrated Mass for the parish on August 8th, 1869, and afterwards announced that he incorporated the sisters into the Dominican Order. Mother Kolumba and her daughters' astonishment and delight could not be described. Fr. Jandel had hardly waited until the Congregation was officially established (by the bishop just that previous January, and by the Galician government in April), before he spiritually adopted it as "Dominican." This left the Congregation independent in operation, but affirmed its Dominican nature.

Fr. Jandel's quickness to affiliate the sisters with the Order of Preachers was more than an expression of his affection for Mother Kolumba. Rather, the Master General who had struggled at length to revitalize and reform the Order of Preachers was gratified to find in this Polish village a healthy sprout of Dominican life. For all the brevity of her formation in Nancy, Mother Kolumba had clearly absorbed and transmitted the Dominican spirituality. From the beginning, Fr. Jandel had perceived that the little woman would be no Dominican in name only: "a love for the Order...lit up her face and made her capable of everything when the advantage of the Order was at stake."[113] She passed on her Dominican heritage with a passion, regarding it as a precious gift and reminding her sisters of such.

Evidently, Fr. Jandel was highly confident of the Dominican character of this Congregation. An indication of this is found in the trust with which Fr. Jandel honored Mother Kolumba in 1871. Returning to Poland for an official visitation of the Dominicans under him, Fr. Jandel asked Mother Kolumba to be his translator: he knew no

---

[113] Cormier, 338.

Polish, but she could speak French.[114] Since the Dominican priests of the area resisted Fr. Jandel's efforts of reform, they had tended to show coolness towards the Sisters of St. Dominic, but Mother Kolumba did not let this deter her from connecting with her Dominican family— even when money was most tight, she had shared her "widow's mite" with the nuns in Kraków. Now, serving as a translator called for great diplomacy to convey Fr. Jandel's corrections to the nuns. What is more, Fr. Jandel's request for her to translate spoke loudly of his trust that she could understand and convey what was most important to him.

Of primary importance to Fr. Jandel was the belief that adhering to traditional Dominican practices was both possible and the path to holiness. Whereas some confreres held that the rules were outdated or simply impossible for modern man, Fr. Jandel argued that the Dominican constitutions had come from a saint, had earned the approval of the holy Church, had created outstanding saints, and needed to be tried on their own terms before they were modified or dismissed. Initially, Fr. Jandel himself had disliked many of the customs, but he came to believe that holiness was to be found in their observance.[115]

Some of the customs that Fr. Jandel emphasized—such as perpetual abstinence from meat and praying Matins in the wee hours—were never a rule for the Sisters of St. Dominic. But the spirit behind them was undoubtedly alive in Mother and revealed in other practices planted in the Congregation. For example, the Master General argued that ongoing study was both indispensable and compatible with regular prayer; scheduled prayer, in fact, reinforced the self-discipline

---

[114] Cf. Mazur, 28-9.

[115] All information on Fr. Jandel's view of reform taken from *The Life of Alexandre-Vincent Jandel, O.P.*, by Bl. Hyacinth Cormier, O.P.

so beneficial to study.[116] Mother Kolumba similarly valued study and expected daily spiritual reading, while also holding her sisters to a regular schedule of prayer in common. She clearly did not consider study and prayer to be in conflict, but to be mutually beneficial.

One practice that Fr. Jandel prioritized was that of regular "chapter" meetings to address shortcomings within the community. From the earliest days, Dominicans had adopted the monastic practice of admitting their own faults and receiving reprimand from their brothers in community meetings. A Dominican is expected not so much to be perfect, as to be an imperfect human who constantly desires to improve.[117] Mother Kolumba understood the importance of such chapters and made them a practice among the sisters, expecting them to apologize regularly as well as to receive correction in chapter meetings. In fact, she emphasized that this was so important to the sisters' growth in holiness that a superior who failed to hold the chapters with weekly regularity might be removed from her office.[118] This underscored vigilance to keep either laxity or sin from taking root in the community—or in the individual sister.

Dominicans consider their life to be one of constantly forming oneself to be more like Christ. Equally indispensable as ongoing study is mortification: as Jesus said, "Whoever does not carry the cross and follow me cannot be my disciple."[119] This cross can take many forms, and a life committed to carrying it can go under many names, such as "penance," "asceticism," or "self-denial." All of these imply the hardship involved in transforming our sinful selves and turning towards virtue. Christians have to constantly respond to God's grace, saying "no" to

---

[116] Cormier, 206f.

[117] Cf. *Book of Customs*, 133.

[118] See *Constitutions of 1888*, XV, para. 60 and *Book of Customs*, para. 135.

[119] Luke 14:27.

their selfish inclinations and "yes" to opportunities to go beyond, and this is far from easy.

In notes from her spiritual diary, one can see how Mother Kolumba struggled with such sacrifices herself. Sometimes she felt apathetic about her life and responsibilities to a point resembling depression. "They seem so trivial to me and so heavy," she wrote... "as if nothing more were of interest in my life."[120] This was likely compounded by her relentless tuberculosis: "In my soul I have feelings of abandonment, such tiredness, and from outside I am overwhelmed by physical weakness." She described having a sense of "spiritual lethargy," and the further complication that, as Mother General, she had no superior to whom she could confide her troubles.

But meditation made Mother Kolumba realize that "the direct means of helping carry this cross" should be her faith. Faith called to mind "the love and sacrifice of the God-Man. He not only was not tired and fed up with His hardships and difficulties during the thirty-three years of His life, but He desired to prolong that life until the end of centuries so that He could sacrifice Himself for us in the Mystery of the Altar...So He established this Sacrament of His Godly love, [the Eucharist]...This is a model [for me]."[121] Once again, Mother Kolumba turned to the Eucharist for her inspiration, this time to help her deal with specific internal and external difficulties. In prayer and acceptance of mortification "which stem from faith"[122], she found unity with Christ.

Such an "inner spirit" was what Mother Kolumba named as necessary to sustain her sisters. In addition to faith and prayer, the sisters

---

120 This and following taken from *Spiritual Inspirations*, July 26, 1882.

121 Ibid. Underline added.

122 *Directory for the Novitiate*, 23.

123 *Directory for the Novitiate*, 23.

must cultivate a spirit of mortification.[123] Able to speak from her own struggles, Mother Kolumba urged sisters to not waste any opportunity to "tolerate willingly every day's crosses and unpleasant incidents"[124] —this was the way to become like Christ. The usual Lenten fasts, for instance, were to be combined with "all tribulations, sorrow, shortages, and adversities, etc." in one sacrifice to the Lord.[125] Rather than recommend hairshirts or still stiffer mortifications, Mother Kolumba focused on the internal change desired: "work persistently and humbly over yourself; leave behind the previous person you used to be and transform into a new person."[126]

In the battle between various sinful tendencies and transformation into a new person, it can seem as though some part of oneself is dying. Mother Kolumba was familiar with Dominican mystics such as Johannes Tauler, who described this life-transformation in radical language of death. Like Tauler, Mother Kolumba spoke of overcoming sin in oneself as "annihilation" or "crucifying the old self."[127] She was adopting a long Dominican tradition of contemplating and imitating Christ crucified,[128] but she did not mean literally carrying a cross, as the Dominican Rose of Lima had done. Mother Kolumba did not encourage the severe physical disciplines that had long been popular religious practices. She focused more on the internal difficulties of practicing virtue in one's everyday obligations, suggesting, for example, that sisters offer a spiritual sacrifice to the Christ Child at Christmas, such as a resolution "to do better and get rid of some weaknesses [or a]

---

[124] Letter to Sisters Rajmunda and Jacynta on their collecting mission in Zakopane, July 13, 1871.

[125] Letter of [March] 1882.

[126] Letter to Sisters in Wielkie Oczy, Dec. 13, 1872.

[127] Cf. Bakalarz, 103f.

[128] Cf. Bakalarz, 14f.

promise to practice a virtue, etc."[129] Beyond special occasions, Mother expected sisters to pursue perfection through daily sacrifices of duty.

While such sacrifice is mandatory for any disciple of Christ, Mother made it clear that an inner spirit of mortification was indispensable to a sister's apostolate.[130] Even elderly and ill sisters could participate in the Congregation's mission by sacrificing their crosses daily. They could be like their cloistered counterparts, the nuns who supported the Preachers' ministry through prayer and fasting from day one. But active sisters needed to pray and fast as well, so that grace could speak through everything they did—like St. Dominic and his brethren, who sometimes converted heretics simply through their joyful austerity. Without this interior connection to Christ and his saving mission, a sister should not expect her exterior works to yield fruit. She might be surprised, Mother warned, to find herself showing up empty-handed before God's throne![131]

On the other hand, the sisters could participate in the salvation of others' souls—and not overlook their own!—through sacrificial commitment to their daily duties. By accepting hardships in reparation to God "for their own sins and for the sins of those to whom they are sent,"[132] they followed the long tradition of Dominican Third Orders who included "Penance" along with "Dominic" in their name. The sisters considered reparation for sins and self-mortification to be essential for their own salvation and others'. Through their sacrifices, they imitated St. Dominic and St. Catherine of Siena, who did penance for their own sins and pled with God on behalf of others.

The salvation of souls was the original and ultimate aim of the

---

[129] Letter to Sisters in Tyczyn, Dec. 25, 1882.

[130] She especially linked it to their activity of serving the sick, see *Directory for the Novitiate*, 13.

[131] Cf. *Directory for the Novitiate*, 23f.

[132] *Constitutions of 2020*, para. 12.

Order of Preachers; St. Dominic and his friars did everything to save souls. One uniqueness of their constitutions was that it regulated everything to serve this purpose. Mother Kolumba did the same when she maintained some traditional practices, such as public apologies, but did not adopt others—such as praying Matins at a time that would prevent a full night's sleep. Everything was thoughtfully calibrated so as to serve the sisters' mission, while maintaining the value of sacrifice.

But perhaps Mother's most persuasive argument for sacrifice was tied to the sisters' identity as brides of Christ. She viewed the sisters' vows as a total sacrifice of themselves, like the burnt holocausts of old. Therefore, sisters were to hold nothing back from serving Christ. "It would be a shame if religious people avoided mortification," she wrote, "…Oh, who will share the pains and suffering of Jesus Christ if not souls devoted and married to Him!"[133] Both because of their religious consecration and because of their Dominican identity, Mother Kolumba emphasized that the sisters should be characterized by a spirit of mortification. This, along with the spirit of faith and devotion to the Church's mission of salvation, should "enliven" the Sisters of St. Dominic "and constitute their main vow." [134]

And why does a sister make vows? In the Congregation of the Sisters of St. Dominic, two reasons given in their profession are "to imitate Jesus Christ more faithfully" and "to pursue perfect love." Mother Kolumba did not hesitate to link these to reasons to suffer: "we are to practice mortification of the flesh … for the love of the Lord Jesus."[135] In one of her earliest letters, she underscored a lesson from Fr. Leszczyński: sisters, most of all, who have been chosen "to be the

---

[133] Letter of [March] 1882.

[134] *Directory for the Novitiate*, 10.

[135] Letter of [March] 1882.

Brides of the Lord's Son Himself…should place abundant sacrifices at His Divine Feet to demonstrate to our Lord that we love Him with our heart, not only with word but with deed."[136] More prosaically put: say you love God through your actions, not just in words.

No one who knew Mother Kolumba could doubt that she loved God, nor that she loved her Dominican heritage. The customs she bequeathed, from prayer to study to sacrifice, were carefully adopted from her Dominican forebears to guide the sisters in pursuit of perfect love. The spirits of faith and mortification that characterized them were the same that Fr. Jandel had urged as essential to life as Third Order Dominicans—in fact, for any Christian seeking perfection.[137] Fr. Jandel found strength and comfort in Mother Kolumba's commitment to Dominican life, and reciprocated in every way he could, even asking the Pope's blessing upon the Congregation and arranging permission for them to expose the Blessed Sacrament.[138] Between Fr. Jandel and Mother Kolumba, there was undoubtedly a mutual delight: the love of Dominican life.

---

[136] Letter to Sisters Rajmunda and Jacynta on their collecting mission in Hungary, Nov. 4 {1868}.

[137] See Cormier's summary of Fr. Jandel's additions to the Manual for the Third Order— noting that this is directed to laity, not religious sisters, but it is "the same for Christian perfection" [of anyone], Cormier, 116f. We do not know whether Mother Kolumba ever read this Manual, but she clearly held to the same principles as those Cormier outlines: the spirit of faith, the spirit of mortification, and frequent reception of Holy Communion.

[138] Mazur, 28-9.

Chapter 7
A SIMPLE SERVANT

At last the day had come for the chapel to be consecrated and the sisters to move into the completed convent—September 14, 1870. The sisters spent the preceding night in prayer and song in the new chapel, and the next morning Mother Kolumba exhorted them with tears in her eyes: What a life they must lead, now that they were going to live under one roof with the Lord Jesus![139] A lofty calling, this! Who could model such a life for the sisters? Mother Kolumba never presented herself as a model; rather, she taught that the model superior for religious life was Jesus' mother Mary, the one who had first shared a roof with and devoted her life to him.

The tiny foundress had an immense devotion to the Mother of God, so deep that she did not fathom it until the day of her death. Then she exclaimed, "Oh, I did not know I loved the Mother of God so much…I love her so much!"[140] The devotion to which Mother Kolumba was blind was hardly hidden from those around her: she had dedicated not only the chapel in Wielowieś, but the entire

---

[139] *Life*, Ch. X.
[140] *Life*, Ch. XXXII.

Congregation to Mary under the title of her Immaculate Conception. She had already stressed that honoring Mary should be one of the hallmarks of the Congregation. The sisters began their prayers through Mary's intercession in the morning, and concluded them with a hymn to her at night. The Angelus, rosary, Salve Regina and other Marian prayers punctuated the rest of the day, while Saturday was marked with additional honors for Our Lady. Mother especially recommended the rosary as a treasure of the Dominican heritage, but also as "one of the most solid devotions," as it links Mary to Jesus, "through whom alone this Mother of God is everything."[141] She made clear that her devotion to Mary always had Christ as its reason and aim. In this vein, many of Mother Kolumba's sacrifices were offered to Jesus through Mary. She frequently mentioned Our Lady of Sorrows, among all other titles of Mary, perhaps because she found there a model for sharing in Christ's sufferings. Yet suffering in love was not all that this most superior mother could teach the sisters. Simplicity, humility, devoted service to Christ's mission, mature freedom: all of these are characteristics of the consecrated life which Mother Kolumba stressed, and in which her life echoed the Blessed Virgin's.

Simplicity is a virtue which draws upon many others while remaining true to itself. Perhaps its most prominent version is honesty, being transparently true about oneself. "Behold, the handmaid of the Lord," is how Mary presented herself in all simplicity. The rest of us can say, "Behold, the sinner." In fact, Mother Kolumba struggled sometimes to relate to Mary "who was the most innocent and holy of all innocent souls,"[142] because Mother Kolumba knew herself to be a sinner. At times, she labored under regret for sins that seemed

---

[141] *Directory for the Novitiate,* 95.

[142] Paraphrasing *Spiritual Inspirations,* March 1886.

The convent in Wielowieś, pictured 1893, and the chapel's altar as it appeared in Mother's day.

like wicked crimes; at other times, she struggled to evoke enough contrition. But Mother Kolumba never hesitated to approach God in all authenticity, even in view of her own sinfulness—especially through the intercession of Mary, "Refuge of Sinners".

Simple frankness with God characterized the practices of prayer which Mother Kolumba encouraged in her sisters. "Tell the Lord Jesus

The central image and inscription of the chapel (pictured today) proclaim the Congregation's devotion to Our Lady. Inset, the face of the image.

everything your heart dictates," she advised. "He wants no flowery words. Oh, no: [what] he appreciates most is the simplicity of your heart."[143] In all her instructions to reflect on one's shortcomings in meditation, to examine one's conscience—at least twice daily, for seven and ten minutes—and to explicitly seek help in graces from God, there is never a note of holding back. God already knows us thoroughly, it is true, but we need to acknowledge the truth on our part.

Simplicity extends to one's relationships with others as well. Since

---

[143] *Directory for the Novitiate*, 90.

superiors serve as God's delegate, sisters were to be utterly frank with superiors for the sake of their spiritual growth.[144] As mentioned above, sisters were also to meekly receive corrections from each other, and even to ask sisters to bring faults to their attention so as to better know themselves and "live in the truth".[145] Such practices allow a sister to be aware of her real identity, not shy away from shortcomings, and so develop and flourish in God's grace.

Mary's simplicity allowed her to claim nothing more than God's servant as her identity. Similarly, simplicity made Mother Kolumba, who had a rare talent for leading others, avoid all honors possible. She never allowed the sisters to address her as "Most Reverend Mother," as was customary, either in person or in letter. When she had business outside the Congregation, she would sometimes hide the cross worn around her neck, which identified her as a Mother Superior, and charge her companion not to give her away. "However," her secretary recalled, this "did not really work, because either priests or nuns recognized her to be a very special person and they insisted on inquiring as to what function she held in the Congregation." Eventually, the truth must come out—to Mother Kolumba's regret, although she also expressed how hard it was to avoid lying while concealing her true role![146] But Mother's motive was humility; as she instructed her sisters, a superior should leave behind all proud appearance to the point of being

---

[144] Even when at a distance, Mother expected her sisters to share with her via letter about the state of their souls, their inner disposition, meditations, and more. See Letter to Sisters in Wielkie Oczy, Dec. 13, 1872, where she rebukes a sister for not writing to Mother as she was obliged to do.

[145] *Book of Customs,* 442.

[146] *Life,* Ch. XXVI.

[147] See her "Last Testament," *Life,* Ch. XXX.

indistinguishable from the others.[147]

From her childhood, Kolumba Białecka had tried to stay in the background; this humility caused a later acquaintance to remark to the sisters, "Your Mother would like to hide herself somewhere under the ground."[148] But even her natural shyness did not keep Mother Kolumba from leading the way. Like Mary at Cana, she missed nothing and did not fail to direct any sister towards the right path— even if just by a look.[149] While she regularly asked younger sisters for their input on decisions, this did not diminish her dignity. Instead, one sister recalled, such inquiries "humbled us as we felt that we could not equal Mother in anything."[150] But when Mother asked a sister to do something, she imparted so much confidence that the sister felt most able to do the task.[151]

Mother Kolumba encouraged humility and simplicity in her sisters by telling them to decline customary honors of the time, such receiving a gentleman's kiss on one's hand as greeting. One did not become a Sister of St. Dominic to receive honors or enjoy luxuries. So, too, sisters were to cook for themselves simple food—tasty and healthy, but simple. Pickiness was not appropriate for religious women: "even if something goes wrong, involuntarily," Mother wrote, "for instance, the meat is bad, a sister should accept it and not demonstrate her dissatisfaction."[152] Mother advised another sister not to differ from her companion in terms of food. If her sister took coffee, she should as well—"why make others pay attention to you?"[153] A sister should not

---

[148] *Life*, Ch. XXVI.

[149] *Life*, Ch. XXVI.

[150] *Life*, Ch. XXVI.

[151] *Life*, Ch. XXVI.

[152] Letter of [March] 1882.

[153] Letter to Sisters Rajmunda and Joanna on their collecting mission in Hungary, May 11, 1868.

On outings, Mother Kolumba sometimes hid the cross which distinguished her as
Mother Superior of the Congregation.

draw attention herself, but draw others to Christ.

Mary was exemplary at drawing others to Christ, an operation
which she continues to carry out in heaven. In this, the missions
of Mary and the Sisters of St. Dominic coincide with that of the
whole Church: bringing the good news of Christ to all nations. This
coincidence is no accident since St. Dominic formed his Order to

serve the Church. His life shouted allegiance, respect, and love to the Church's representatives. No less was expected from the Sisters of St. Dominic. Mother Kolumba modeled this in every interaction with clergymen, and told the sisters that their job was not only to help the local pastors in their ministry, but even to ease tensions that might occur between them and their flock. Like Mary to her Son, they were to be mediators between people and priest.

The sisters' imitation of Mary was not to end there. The woman addressed as "full of grace" was open to God's demands and responded in true freedom: "Let it be done unto me according to Thy Word."[154] Similarly, the sisters were to open themselves to grace through their committed spiritual life, and never close themselves off to demands which arose from their mission. Mother Kolumba characterized the desired spirit as one of "love, simplicity and freedom"[155]; she intentionally encouraged "the climate of freedom and openness to grace" which was a characteristic of Dominican communities.[156]

Freedom implies a maturity to accept one's responsibilities, and Mother Kolumba tried in every way to raise her daughters to such maturity. She wrote, in her directions for novices, that each daily task should be undertaken with enthusiasm and care, for this would set the tone for every action in their future. They should strive to be simple and humble, responsible and free; loving the Church and committing themselves wholeheartedly to the salvation of their own souls and of others'. Mother Kolumba set an example, but Mary was to be the primary model in consecrating all to God's will.[157]

---

154 Luke 1:28, 38.
155 Letter to Mother Marcelina Darowska, June 6, 1881.
156 Cf. Mazur, 18, where Mazur says she must have absorbed this spirit in Nancy.
157 *Life*, Ch. XXX.

Chapter 8
PURE OBEDIENCE

In order to follow God's will, Mother Kolumba also emphasized the necessity of acting out of obedience and pure intentions. The woman who taught her sisters to preach the Gospel primarily by their lives did not exempt herself from living out what she taught. The harder times of Mother's own life especially illuminate this, such as when Fr. Leszczyński effectively exiled her from the Congregation.

Although she was Superior General of the Congregation, Mother Kolumba lived out obedience in many ways. After obeying Fr. Jandel as though he transmitted the will of God, and submitting herself to her superiors in Nancy, Mother always sought authorization from the bishop and other local authorities for her work. Since the bishop had appointed Fr. Leszczyński to be his vicar over the Congregation, Mother submitted to Father's direction in many domains, even those that were not properly his.

It must be said that Fr. Leszczyński gave his heart and soul to the benefit of the Congregation. Beyond arranging the sisters' welcome in Wielowieś, Father poured himself into the building of their convent, encouraged their unusual apostolate, and supported them against other clergy's antipathy. He truly cared for their souls, saying Mass and hearing Confessions, directing their retreats and writing them letters.

Mother Kolumba rightfully referred to him as the sisters' father, and she always spoke gratefully of all that he did for them. The sisters would show this gratitude, too, as they devoted round-the-clock care to Fr. Leszczyński in his final years.

Unfortunately, however, inescapable differences arose between how Fr. Leszczyński and Mother Kolumba viewed Dominican life, such as how much time the sisters should devote to prayer.[158] These grew along with a cancer on Father's face, which affected his brain and caused irrational thinking. In one case, Father recommended a candidate to the Congregation whom the sisters found unsuitable— but, instead of accepting the decision against admission as properly theirs, Fr. Leszczyński took this as a slight to himself. It loomed large in his mind and became insurmountable, making relations with the sisters ever more difficult.

In addition—and in contrast to the views of the Dominicans who had formed Mother Kolumba—Fr. Leszczyński had a harsh view of human nature. Not uncommon for the time, this led him to impose strict penances and limit reception of Holy Communion. Under obedience to him, Mother Kolumba was kept from receiving Holy Communion for weeks at a time. This was immeasurably painful to her, whose world revolved around the Eucharist!

In virtue of the bishop's appointment to be vicar, Fr. Leszczyński also served as Mother's spiritual director. But, because of their philosophical differences and Father's reasoning being compromised by the cancer, Mother came to a point where she felt that he could not understand her at all. Meetings with him became intimidating; Confession was

---

[158] See Mazur, 36.

equally daunting. What is more, Fr. Leszczyński's interventions made Mother Kolumba unable to direct the Congregation according to her conscience. This caused her great suffering. Mother sought guidance from other priests, yet felt obliged—out of obedience—to return to Fr. Leszczyński's direction.

So, when Fr. Leszczyński suggested that Mother Kolumba spend a stay in Lvov in spring of 1879, she accepted this effective exile. Although Mother ostensibly was sent to Lvov to recover her health, she was aware that her second-in-command, Sister Gertruda, had made plans with Father to take control of the Congregation. But rather than engage in a power struggle, Mother took the time in Lvov to evaluate her understanding of God's plan.

This reevaluation could only have come during a great emotional, physical, and spiritual low. Mother was undoubtedly hurt by Sister Gertruda's disloyalty, as well as by the disrupted relationship with Fr. Leszczyński. Her tuberculosis had significantly worsened over the past winter. She was also in a lonely position in Lvov, separated from her sisters, her life's work, and her longtime spiritual director. Trusty Fr. Jandel could not be turned to for advice, since he had died some years before. As her secretary later summarized, her suffering was so great that "she felt that she could not suffer any more; on the other hand, she thought in humility that Sister Gertruda knew how to substitute for her and govern her Congregation along with Father Leszczyński."[159]

In this humility, Mother Kolumba scrutinized her own role. Rather than cling to the title of Superior General or to her vision of the Congregation, she questioned whether she was meant to lead the sisters at all. Mother had frequently urged the sisters to follow God's will, not for their own benefit or recognition, but for purer intentions:

---

[159] *Life,* Ch. XIV.

"only for the glory of the Lord Jesus, to fulfill His Holy Will and to ensure salvation of souls."[160] She admonished against doing anything for financial or worldly benefits, much less showing preference between those who asked for their help.[161] Other ulterior motives must also be resisted: "be watchful lest people's recognition, self-love, or any kind of vanity creep into your intentions while you work in a new position."[162] Mother warned that pride and arrogance could ruin otherwise good actions.[163] Even love needed to be pure: as she wrote to sisters who missed her so much, "ask the Lord Jesus to purify your love for me of any selfishness and make it truly Godly in every aspect…Let us wish only that God's will be realized, as well as the salvation of souls."[164]

Now, Mother Kolumba considered whether she was called to humbly step out of leadership and enter a cloistered community. After all, the cloistered life had attracted Mother Kolumba from the very beginning, and there she would be able to truly devote herself to worship of the Eucharist. In her loneliness, Mother Kolumba was attacked by scruples of conscience. Had she originally mistaken God's vocation for her? Had she been pursuing her own visions instead of His? She resolved to leave the Congregation in God's hands and enter a cloistered convent in Gródek, Kraków. To do this with due obedience, Mother Kolumba asked the bishop for permission. She did not divulge all of the reasons for her decision because she was reluctant to cast Fr. Leszczyński in a bad light. The bishop willingly gave his consent, but Providence intervened. Fr. Łobos, the bishop's spokesman and a friend to Mother, was inspired to add to the bishop's letter: "we consider the

[160] Letter to an unidentified sister, September 1886.

[161] *Life*, Ch. XXX.

[162] Letter to an unidentified sister, September 1886.

[163] Cf. Letter to Sister Dominika in Lvov, [June 1878].

[164] Letter to Sisters in Wielkie Oczy, July 28, 1879.

Fr. Jósef Weber   Fr. Ignacy Łobos

Fr. Ignacy Łobos and Fr. Jósef Weber—both later made bishops—gave Mother Kolumba invaluable advice. Fr. Weber became her spiritual director and, in 1881, became spiritual director of the Congregation as well. He guided the Sisters for 25 years until he resigned from his positions to enter the Resurrectionist order.

Congregation established in our Diocese by your zeal and great sacrifice to be not firm enough to exist without you and unable to develop in the spirit of St. Dominic the Patriarch, in which you are completely immersed, without your motherly protection. …If you were willing to consider sacrificing your health and life for this Congregation which is your offspring—and needs, we believe, your heart and toil"—the bishop would greet a change of mind with gladness.[165]

Totally blindsided by this message, Mother visited the bishop's office to ask whether any outside party had intervened in the matter. No, Fr. Łobos explained: when composing the bishop's answer,

[165] *Life*, Ch. XV.

"these were the thoughts that came to my mind, and I could not write anything else but only what was written."[166] Taking this to be an expression of God's will, Mother Kolumba revealed all of her difficulties. With all due respect to Fr. Leszczyński, Mother explained that she could not act in spiritual freedom nor lead the Congregation according to her conscience. In response, the bishop's spokesman told Mother Kolumba to act freely in regards to both her soul and to the Congregation. She was also encouraged to continue spiritual direction with Fr. Józef Weber, a seminary professor in Lvov to whom she had turned before.

It is worth considering whether Mother's new resolution to lead the Congregation wasn't harder than the first. Fr. Łobos was not speaking lightly when he wrote of the Congregation taking the sacrifice of Mother's health and life. Her tuberculosis only sporadically remitted, she had to return to the problems of governing a newborn congregation and dealing with a sister-vicar who had caused great division. But Mother Kolumba lived out what she had succinctly expressed: "Where our superiors place us, God's will wants us there."[167] Now that her superiors had indicated Mother should lead the Congregation, she obeyed with the purest of intentions: to fulfill God's will.

---

[166] *Life*, Ch. XV.
[167] Letter to Sister Alana in Wielkie Oczy, May 4, 1874.

Chapter 9
CONSTITUTIONAL HEALTH

In addition to her vocational ups and downs, Mother Kolumba bore many other burdens as well. Within one year, she lost both of her biological sisters, and the premature deaths of several religious sisters were a sorrow that never left her.[168] Added to her own lifelong struggle with tuberculosis, this made mortality no stranger to Mother Kolumba. In fact, it's a testament to Róża Białecka's character that sickness did not dominate her life entirely. The tuberculosis that plagued her from her youth would have kept many other genteel women confined to bed, and certainly nipped in the bud any ideas of starting a religious institution from nothing! Instead, Mother Kolumba took still more active measures to ensure that the Congregation would be preserved beyond her lifetime. In early 1885, she resolved to travel to Rome to expedite approval of the Congregation's constitutions.

The lengthy trip by cart, bus, and train was no light undertaking for such an ill woman. The sisters worried that their Mother may not return to them alive: it was, after all, midwinter. But Mother had just

---

[168] In the papal audience in 1885, when Pope Leo XIII asked Mother how numerous the Congregation was, she lamented that 12 sisters had already died.

completed a two-and-a-half-month medical treatment in Lvov, and wanted to take advantage of the small improvement in health that it brought her. Mother Kolumba had no illusions that she would live much longer, but hoped that the Holy See would crown her life's work by setting its seal of approval on the constitutions.

The first constitutions of the Sisters of St. Dominic were those which Mother brought from the Dominican sisters in Nancy and translated into Polish. As Bishop Jasiński had advised, the first sisters had operated under these constitutions and adapted them before submitting them for diocesan approval in 1867. An official decree of establishment had come from the diocese in 1868, and approval from the Galician government that same year. In 1874, the bishop had approved new laws for the Congregation, written with an eye to the relationship between the motherhouse and mission houses.

These revisions were a happy necessity, since the Congregation was already expanding. Increasing demand for the sisters' work outpaced the number of incoming candidates. Thanks to fundraising forays in nearby Bieliny, the sisters had been asked to bring their apostolate there. After visiting for catechesis for stretches of time, the sisters moved into a private home in Bieliny in 1871, and rejoiced in a completed convent five years later. In 1872, eleven years after their start in Wielowieś, they had accepted an invitation to settle in Wielkie Oczy. But unhealthy housing conditions, the unreliability of local authorities, and a fickle patroness caused that branch to close within a few years. Promising invitations arose elsewhere and a more sustainable outpost was begun in Tyczyn in 1878. A fourth house would be opened in Rawa Ruska in 1886, and property in Biala Nizna was already promised, although it would not come into the Congregation's possession until 1895.

With multiple houses and local authorization, the Congregation

The Congregations' ministry quickly expanded to Biała Niżna (top) and Rawa Ruska (middle). Both the convents built in Biała Niżna and Bieliny (bottom) still house the sisters.

was undoubtedly in good standing, but Mother Kolumba set her sights on approval from the Holy See. Becoming a pontifical institute would ensure that the Congregation could operate independently of any one bishop's approval and would allow the Congregation to easily expand its evangelization to any diocese. While Mother Kolumba was passionate about helping the poor of her nation, she was a true daughter of Dominic. She did not focus only on a small group of people, but desired the Gospel to be preached to all in need. Despite tuberculosis treatments, she overhauled the constitutions with Fr. Weber's help. This revision the bishop approved in 1883. Mother then translated the new constitutions into French so that they could be sent to Rome for review.

The revised constitutions reflected some lessons taught by time: having seen many of her sisters depleted by work and taken by illness, for example, Mother chose to reduce how often they fasted. Mother Kolumba treasured her daughters' good health— frequently advising the sisters to take precautions to preserve it and arranging dispensations to lighten tolls on their health. "If you love me," she once wrote, like any mother using her relationship to rouse guilt, "then you will watch over your health."[169] As the case may be, she would urge her sisters to take contemporary measures such as drinking milk or wine, eating plenty of grapes, and—for heaven's sake!—don't hesitate to call the doctor! In the same breath, she would assure her sisters not to worry about herself, "I have a piece of the left lung left; I can still live with that for the next several years...So be calm."[170] Mother Kolumba downplayed her own health so much that Fr. Jandel once called her

---

[169] Letter to Sisters Rajmunda and Jacynta on their collecting mission in Hungary, [Sep. 1871].

[170] Letter to an unidentified sister in Rawa Ruska, [January 1887].

The ailing foundress was
determined to travel to Rome.

"incorrigible" for giving him no news of it.[171]

Whereas the sisters' health was so precious that Mother Kolumba
would spare no expense[172], she resisted doctors' advice for her to spend
the winter of 1869-70 away from Wielowieś, arguing that it was not
in keeping with a vow of poverty to adopt such expensive measures.
The "incorrigible" woman insisted that she would give herself home
treatments instead![173] In desperation, the sisters turned to Fr. Jandel,
using his timely visit to convince Mother Kolumba to stay in a balmier
climate. Viewing his wish as an order to be obeyed, Mother agreed to
winter in Cette, France. With everything thoughtfully arranged by Fr.
Jandel, Mother Kolumba was also able to visit holy places such as the
cave at Marseille of Mary Magdalene, patroness of the Dominican

[171] Cormier, 340.

[172] See Letter to Sisters Rajmunda and Jacynta on their collecting mission in Zakopane,
July 13, 1871.

[173] *Life*, Ch. IX.

Order, and Rome, Assisi, and St. Dominic's tomb in Bologna.

This stay away improved Mother's health, but the tuberculosis was never in remission for long. The swampy area around Wielowieś only encouraged it; although Mother Kolumba repeatedly went for treatments in Lvov, she knew that it was only a matter of time before the tuberculosis won out. So she resolutely set out for Rome in January 1885 to resolve this business of papal approval as soon as possible.

Fr. Jandel, who had headquartered in Rome, had passed away in 1872, but Mother Kolumba made use of every other connection she had to hasten the approval of the Congregation's constitutions. Her diplomatic presence paid off: in late March, the Holy See issued a Laudatory Decree, officially praising the sisters' work. This wasn't quite final approval, but it was a feather in one's cap: the Laudatory Decree even praised the sisters' catechetical work that had received criticism from other quarters.[174] Before the constitutions were fully approved, the Holy See suggested some small modifications to be made and Mother Kolumba returned home, confident that the road forward lay clear.

Mother Kolumba's life work—or rather, the fruits of her responsiveness to God's plan—stood in good shape. Despite tuberculosis and her share of sorrows, Mother had fought on bravely. She had taught her daughters that physical health is important, but more valuable still is one's spiritual welfare. She had set the example of perseverance through suffering, established her daughters in a life of virtues and time-tested Rules, and could see the Congregation slowly but surely expanding. The little foundress, who sought to provide everything prudent for her daughters' future, knew she had only a few more tasks before she could rest in peace.

---

[174] See Bakalarz, p. 117 and note 708.

Chapter 10
PROVIDING FOR ANY NEED

"Happy the one who has St. Joseph as patron" runs a hymn which the sisters sang to St. Joseph. Out of all her devotions, Mother Kolumba passed on to the sisters a daily prayer to St. Joseph. Through it, sisters ask St. Joseph to provide all that they need, spiritually and materially, to fulfill their vocations as daughters of St. Dominic. For any need, Mother Kolumba encouraged confidence in this guardian of the Christ Child and of virgins, who is also the patron saint for a happy death. As Mother Kolumba drew near to her own last days, she underscored what she had long advised: to spend each day in light not just of death, but of eternity.

Religious life is lived as a reminder of eternity: the consecrated woman forsakes everything to be the bride of Christ, adopting the role which all Christians are destined to take in Heaven. Mother Kolumba had regularly added weight to her exhortations to sisters by recalling that they were to live as Brides of Christ—even though Mother herself had once confided that she never called Jesus her Bridegroom because she felt unworthy.[175] Indeed, in Mother Kolumba's eyes, this supernatural vocation was no reason to tout oneself, but to more perfectly prepare for eternity.

As 1886 drew to an end, Mother Kolumba knew that eternity was approaching her. She had visited several specialists who extended her life through treatments but predicted she would not live many more months. Mother made her goodbyes to friends in Lvov, visited her elderly mother one last time, and returned to Wielowieś for Christmas. But for the first time, she was too weak to join the sisters for Christmas celebrations. On Epiphany, she resolved one matter that had long weighed upon her: she appointed a sister to succeed her as novice mistress.

Mother Kolumba's life was touch-and-go throughout January and February. When some junior sisters renewed their vows in early February, all knew with sorrow that it was the last time such vows would be made in Mother Kolumba's hands. During one close call about this time, Fr. Weber had a dream that "someone told me clearly, 'Mother will die on the 18th.'"[176] But he reminded the sisters that dreams were only that; as February 18th came and went, it seemed that they should put no stock in his strange premonition.

Meanwhile, Mother's physical suffering was immense—a doctor said that only 1% of tuberculosis victims reacted so severely as she. But Mother resisted taking medication for the pain because she did not want to miss the chance to sacrifice. Knowing that the pain of her illness could cause great irritability, Mother Kolumba did fear that she would lose her patience, but her companion recorded that "not the slightest sign of irritation could be detected [in her]. The heartlessness

---

[175] *Life*, Ch. XXVI.
[176] *Life*, Ch. XXXI.

and indifference towards everything which are typical for this illness did not appear in Mother at all."[177] Instead, "[s]he was constantly concentrating upon Holy God and us; consequently, even the doctors could not conceal their admiration."[178] Mother's gentleness and gratitude during this time also impressed the sisters.

Not trusting her own example to be enough, Mother Kolumba used every opportunity and ounce of energy to impress virtue upon her sisters. She called older sisters to her bedside and imparted final wisdom to them, reminding them that "within a few years, many of you could become superiors," and they must pass on her lessons to the younger sisters.[179] Pure intentions, humility, sisterly love, suitable relationships with priests and laity, obedience—these were the topics of one morning's instructions. Not satisfied to leave it at that, Mother summoned the sisters back in the afternoon and spoke of devotion to the Eucharist and to Mary; love and unity; and again humility. The sisters put her valuable words into writing, intending to inscribe them into their lives as well.

Some days later, Mother Kolumba reminded the older sisters of the importance of obedience to her successor, to the Holy Spirit, to the constitutions, and to Fr. Weber (now the Congregation's spiritual director). She reiterated some of her earlier points and reminded the sisters to be faithful to their meditation. "[If you] go into this exercise with the desire to know the will of God…it will be clear: this is bad, and this is good!"[180] Such were the contents of her last will and testament to her daughters.

March came, with Mother still suffering, and the sisters began

---

[177] *Life,* Ch. XXXI.
[178] *Life,* Ch. XXXI.
[179] *Life,* Ch. XXX.
[180] *Life,* Ch. XXX.

their annual novena to St. Joseph—this time, mainly for the intention of graces for their beloved Superior General. Mother Kolumba asked to have a small altar in her room decorated for St. Joseph, and for the novena to be said for her to have a happy death on St. Joseph's feast day (March 19th) or its eve. "She trusted that, through St. Joseph's intercession, she would receive that grace."[181] As the feast grew closer, Mother's suffering intensified: a high fever continued without any break, and such ulcers covered her throat that Mother Kolumba was unable to swallow, not even a teaspoonful of water.

Her fever combined with her devotion made her resemble a Eucharistic lamp even more. One sister recorded:

> Inside and out, she burned like a sanctuary light full of love for her Heavenly Bridegroom. She said the Novena to St. Joseph zealously and desired to pass away on the Eve or the day of his Feast. However, she submitted herself to God's will and she wished to suffer even more. What proved most painful to Beloved Mother was that during this week she could not receive Holy Communion, but she consoled herself that the Lord would compensate her in another way.[182]

Sleep was elusive, swallowing medicine was impossible. One consolation came in the form of encouraging letters from Fr. Weber, who could not come himself. Mother Kolumba often reread his letters, rejoicing at the spiritual nuggets they held. As death came nearer, Mother Kolumba seemed to have only one worry: that a priest would not be present during her final struggle. She begged and begged for the current pastor of Wielowieś, Fr. Ciechanowicz, to promise his presence.

The attending doctor was Fr. Ciechanowicz's brother, a specialist from Kraków. As March 18th dawned, the eve of St. Joseph's feast, he

---

[181] *Life*, Ch. XXXI.
[182] *Life*, Ch. XXXI.

was called to give help for a particularly bad coughing fit. Aware of Mother's prayer to St. Joseph, he confided to a sister that it seemed her wish would be granted. The sister relayed this to Mother and received a delighted smile as a result. Mother Kolumba clearly awaited death with great desire and peace. But she continued to say, "Whatever is the Lord's will!"[183]

Earlier that day than usual, Mother Kolumba asked sisters to pray with her the novena to St. Joseph, which ended with the song "Happy the one who has St. Joseph as patron…". This time, Mother asked for the song to be repeated; as a sister sang it, she watched Mother raise her eyes in prayer and silently entreat St. Joseph for his care in the hour of her death, and—as he was asked daily—to provide anything that the Congregation might need.

That night, at least the first half of Mother's prayer was answered. At about 9:30 p.m., surrounded by her sisters, Fr. Ciechanowicz, and their prayers, Mother Kolumba passed in total peace. It was the eve of St. Joseph, and Mother Kolumba had suffered so much, her secretary noted, that she was spared further agony. She sighed lightly and was gone. But her foresight continued to provide for the sisters even in their grief: Mother had asked Fr. Ciechanowicz to calm them with consoling words.

Other good souls, too, rallied around the distraught sisters, who felt like bereft orphans. Two villagers traveled through deep snow to bring the government-stipulated coffin. Fr. Weber sent a comforting letter, as well as a short biography written in Latin to be enclosed in the coffin. The local clergy showed their respect by laying out the coffin in great state. And a state marshal went to great lengths to obtain permission for Mother Kolumba to be buried in the garden

---

[183] *Life*, Ch. XXXII.

right behind the chapel.

To that grave, sisters "frequently run…to draw strength in prayer and to not fall under the burden of the cross."[184] Not only the sisters, but many local townspeople—even those of Róża Białecka's childhood home—experience her care well after her death. This should not surprise those who know how Mother Kolumba cared for her sisters and her countrymen; she spared no ounce of attention to provide for them as a mother would.

Mother Kolumba was buried directly behind the convent chapel, near the Blessed Sacrament. Since then, her remains have been transferred to inside the chapel.

---

[184] *Life*, Ch. XXXIII.

A grotto (above) and plaque (right of the grotto) near her birthplace mark the local
Ukrainians' devotion to Mother Kolumba and trust in her intercession.

Epilogue

Near the end of her life, Mother Kolumba asked a favor of her childhood friend. She gave Sister Innocenta a photo of herself and asked her to discreetly burn it in the sanctuary lamp. On the back of the photo, Mother had written a prayer asking that Jesus consume her life so that only his would reign in her. This burnt offering well summarized her life; in the words of her friend Bishop Łobos, Jesus "alloyed her heart to be able to remain in it as though in the tabernacle."[185] The bishop noted that this refining fire came through Mother's sufferings, only a few of which can be named here: homesickness, slander, debilitating health, depression, lack of funds, differences with a priest she revered, uncertainties and doubts. Despite this, Mother Kolumba gave herself completely to serve God's will and to respond to the fire of his love that she found in the Eucharist.

The greatness of a person cannot be summarized by her children, but the lessons imparted are part of her legacy. Thus, much of Mother Kolumba's story has been illustrated by what her sisters learned from her.

One such sister was an orphan girl raised by Mother Kolumba's offspring—Sister Julia Rodzińska—who served as school administrator, orphanage director, and local superior in the town

---

[185] See Mazur, 48, quoting letter from Bishop Łobos of April 1, 1887. This letter is published also in *Misericordias Domini in Aeternum Cantabo*.

Before her arrest, Sister Julia had won accolades and the moniker "Mother of the Orphans" for her work directing an orphanage and other outreach to needy children in Vilnius (now in Lithuania).

of Vilnius. Citizens awarded her accolades for her creative and unsparing work for the poorest children of Vilnius, but after the city was invaded by the Soviets in 1939, the sisters' work was put a stop. Undaunted, Sister Julia joined in underground efforts to pass on the Catholic faith and Polish culture. She also coordinated food for elderly priests who were left without rations, and was involved in the archbishop's efforts to save Jews. In 1943, the Nazis arrested Sister Julia for "political crimes" and kept her in solitary confinement for a year in a prison through which screams of torture rang. All this withstanding, a peace-filled Sister Julia was transferred to Stutthof Concentration Camp, where she was placed in the most ghastly section, that designated for Jewish women.

Sister Julia proved herself to be Mother Kolumba's daughter not just by the works that landed her in Stutthof, but by her actions once she found herself there. She impressed fellow prisoners by her humane and hopeful care for others, her brave and constant prayer, her love of religious life, and her willingness to give anything to have a rosary or receive the Eucharist. In a place where all were stripped of dignity, Sister Julia sought out those most in need. This extended to caring for typhoid victims when an epidemic swept the section. Co-prisoners pleaded with her not to risk her life helping the "typhoid women," but Sister Julia persisted. The fever took her as a result. She died on February 20, 1945, shortly before the camp was liberated. Her self-sacrifice burnt itself into the memory of survivors, who claimed she was a saint; subsequently, John Paul II declared Blessed Julia Rodzińska to be a martyr.

Caring for the sick and needy, persisting despite all struggle and sacrifice, finding hope and strength in prayer—all these and more are ways in which Blessed Julia lived her heritage as a Sister of St.

Dominic. Her heroism in Stutthof highlights the quieter heroism of life which Mother Kolumba modeled for her daughters.

This way of life has spread throughout four continents as the Sisters of St. Dominic have expanded over time. Today, they include over 300 sisters in nine countries, from Canada to Cameroon to Russia's Siberia. In addition to the forms of preaching of Mother's day, the sisters bring the Gospel to the poor, sick, and needy through work in daycares and hospitals, offering retreats, and providing homes for the elderly and mentally disabled.

After Mother Kolumba's death, her beloved spiritual director Fr. Józef Weber continued to give fatherly guidance to the Congregation. A seminary professor at the time, he was later made bishop, then archbishop. All along, Fr. Weber provided assistance to the Congregation, but in 1906, he resigned from this role as well as from the bishopric in order to enter a religious congregation, the Resurrectionists. Archbishop Weber later immigrated to the United States to serve his religious brothers and his Polish countrymen there. Until his death in Chicago in 1918, he kept contact with the Sisters of St. Dominic and urged them to come serve also in America.

The sisters did come to Chicago, but not until some years later. When two did venture across the Atlantic Ocean in 1925, it was on the same sort of fundraising mission for which Mother Kolumba had dispatched sisters in her own day. Then the sisters stayed in Chicago, initially to teach in parishes. Amid ups and downs, they decided to purchase farmland in the village of Justice, some distance outside Chicago. Elderly women began to find a home with them there, and so the sisters' first home for the elderly was born in 1936. Sisters in the Immaculate Conception Province, which includes the U.S. and Canada, continue to preach the Gospel by running a nursing home

After resigning from his archbishopric to enter the Resurrectionists, Józef Weber urged Sisters of St. Dominic to join him catechizing in the United States.

and a preschool, teaching in parishes, hosting retreats, and visiting the sick or homebound.

The flourishing of Mother Kolumba's work and the holiness that shines and hides in various sisters belie what the humble foundress claimed: that she was undeserving of recognition and deserved only oblivion. Although Mother's contemporaries had no doubt of her holiness, the sisters respected her humility by keeping her story to themselves. They did not publicize their Mother Foundress outside of the Congregation, and so almost a century passed before they ever began pursuing a cause for canonization.

The passage of time can make it more difficult to investigate a person's holiness, but evidence abounded for Mother's case. In 2004, John Paul II approved a Decree of Heroic Virtues, declaring that Mother Kolumba can be venerated for the virtues she displayed. In preparation for this decree, nine theologians are appointed by the Vatican to investigate the life of the person in question. At least five must give positive opinions in order for the Decree of Heroic Virtues to be made. In the case of Mother Kolumba, there was no doubt: the vote was unanimous. In addition to the theological and cardinal virtues[186], the theologians specifically named obedience, purity, poverty, and humility as notable in her life.

As of this writing, the process is still underway for Mother Kolumba to be beatified. Official beatification requires that a miracle occur through the venerable person's intercession so as to prove that she is indeed united with God in heavenly glory. While many have recounted graces received through Mother Kolumba's intercession, a demonstrable miracle is harder to prove. Still, whether it be for a need

---

[186] I.e.: faith, hope, and charity (the theological virtues) and prudence, justice, fortitude, and temperance (the cardinal virtues).

large or small, you are encouraged to find help in this holy woman's intercession. The following is a suggested prayer:

Almighty and eternal God, inspired by the example of the Blessed Virgin Mary and nourished with the Most Holy Eucharist, the object of her ardent devotion, your Servant Maria Kolumba Białecka consecrated herself completely to you. Teach me to be like her, open to the prompting of the Holy Spirit as she was, and show me in the example of her life how to grow and persevere in heartfelt piety for the Eucharist and in a childlike love for Mary, the Mother of your Son Jesus. Look upon her sacrificial love for you, and in your great mercy, grant me through her intercession the grace of _____, for which I humbly ask. Amen.

    Our Father…Hail Mary… Glory Be…

If you receive any special graces through Mother Kolumba's help, you are encouraged to share them with the Sisters of St. Dominic by contacting:

    9000 W. 81st Street, Justice, IL, 60458, U.S.A.

    or provincialhouse@sistersop.com

Works Referenced

Bakalarz, O.P., Julia Stanisława. *Contemplation and Action in Mother Kolumba Białecka's Spiritual Life. Kraków,* WAM, 1994. First English edition.

— "Vocation to the Eucharistic Life of the Lord's Servant Mother Kolumba Białecka in Light of Holy Father John Paul II's Teaching of the Eucharist." …So That Christ Could Live within Me from Now On, Symposium of the Congregation of the Sisters of St. Dominic, 11-12 Feb., 2005, Kraków, Keynote Address . First English edition.

Bedouelle, O.P., Guy. *Saint Dominic: The Grace of the Word.* Ignatius Press, 1987.

Congregation of the Sisters of St. Dominic, *Book of Customs,* Kraków, 2007. 2020 English edition.

—*Misericordias Domini in Aeternum Cantabo: Mother Kolumba Białecka at the door of eternity.* Kraków, Publishing House of the Discalced Carmelites, 2007. First English edition.

— "Ratio Formationis," *Give Diligence to Make Your Calling and Choice Certain: Manual of Formation.* Kraków, 2003. First English edition.

Cormier, O.P., Hyacinthe-Marie. *Life of Alexandre-Vincent Jandel, O.P.: Seventy-Third Master General of the Friars Preachers.* Trans. George G. Christian, O.P., and Richard L. Christian. New Priory Press, 2015.

"Galician Slaughter," Wikipedia. 11 June 2020.
https://en.wikipedia.org/wiki/Galician_slaughter

Habsburg, Eduard. "They Did Nothing But Pray." *First Things*. 27 June 2019,
https://www.firstthings.com/web-exclusives/2019/06/they-did-nothing-but-pray.

Kuligowski, Waldemar. "A history of Polish serfdom: Theses and antitheses,"
Eurozine. 13 Feb. 2018, https://www.eurozine.com/a-history-of-polish-serfdom/.

Mazur, O.P., Zygmunt, and Joachim Roman Bar, OFMConv. *Faithful to Hidden
Love.* Kraków, Publishing House of the Discalced Carmelites, 1989.

McNally, S.J., Robert. "The Council of Trent and Vernacular Bibles." N.d. http://
cdn.theologicalstudies.net/27/27.2/27.2.2.pdf.

Pasławska, O.P., Benwenuta. *The Life of Reverend Mother Róża Kolumba Białecka.*
Kraków, Publishing House of the Discalced Carmelites , 2007. 2019
English edition.

Steinig, O.P., Serafina. *Mother Maria Kolumba Białecki: Foundress of Polish
Dominican Sisters,* 1838-1887. Trans. Maria Ferensowicz. Toronto, Century
Publishing, 1983.

"The question of utility: The 'Klostersturm' under Joseph II," The World of the
Habsburgs. 2020, https://www.habsburger.net/en/chapter/question-utility-klostersturm-under-joseph-ii.

Church Documents

Catechism of the Catholic Church. Libreria Editrice Vaticana, © 1994. English
edition available through Doubleday Publishing.

Dei Verbum: Dogmatic Constitution on Divine Revelation, 1965. Available at https://www.vatican.va/archive/hist_councils/ii_vatican_council/documents/vat-ii_const_19651118_dei-verbum_en.html.

Divino Afflante Spiritu: On Promoting Biblical Studies, 1943. Available at http://www.vatican.va/content/pius-xii/en/encyclicals/documents/hf_p-xii_enc_30091943_divino-afflante-spiritu.html.

Publications of Documents Written by Mother Kolumba Białecka

Directory for the Novitiate and Prescriptions for the Filial Houses.

Letters to Sisters Thoughts and Intents of the Heart series. Kraków, Publishing House of the Discalced Carmelites, © Congregation of Sisters of St. Dominic, 2006. First English edition.

Spiritual Inspirations. Thoughts and Intents of the Heart series. Kraków, Publishing House of the Discalced Carmelites, © Congregation of Sisters of St. Dominic, 2008. First English edition.

Sisters in the Immaculate Conception Province (U.S./Canada) celebrate with great joy the final profession of three sisters' vows.

Sisters pray the Liturgy of the Hours together